The Place Between Our Fears

LIFE IN CONGO AND BEYOND

Dawn Hurley
with Mapendo Ndongotsi
and Argentine Imanirakunda

Dawn Hurley
dhurley@shonacongo.com

Publisher's Note: The events, places, and conversations in this memoir have been recreated from our best memories. Some events, individuals, and names have been omitted to respect the privacy of those involved. All the people in this book represent real people. The only names that have been changed are those of Berthe, Bernadette, Chantal, Promesse, and
Chrétien.

The Place Between Our Fears/Hurley -- 1st ed.
ISBN 978-0-578-57615-2

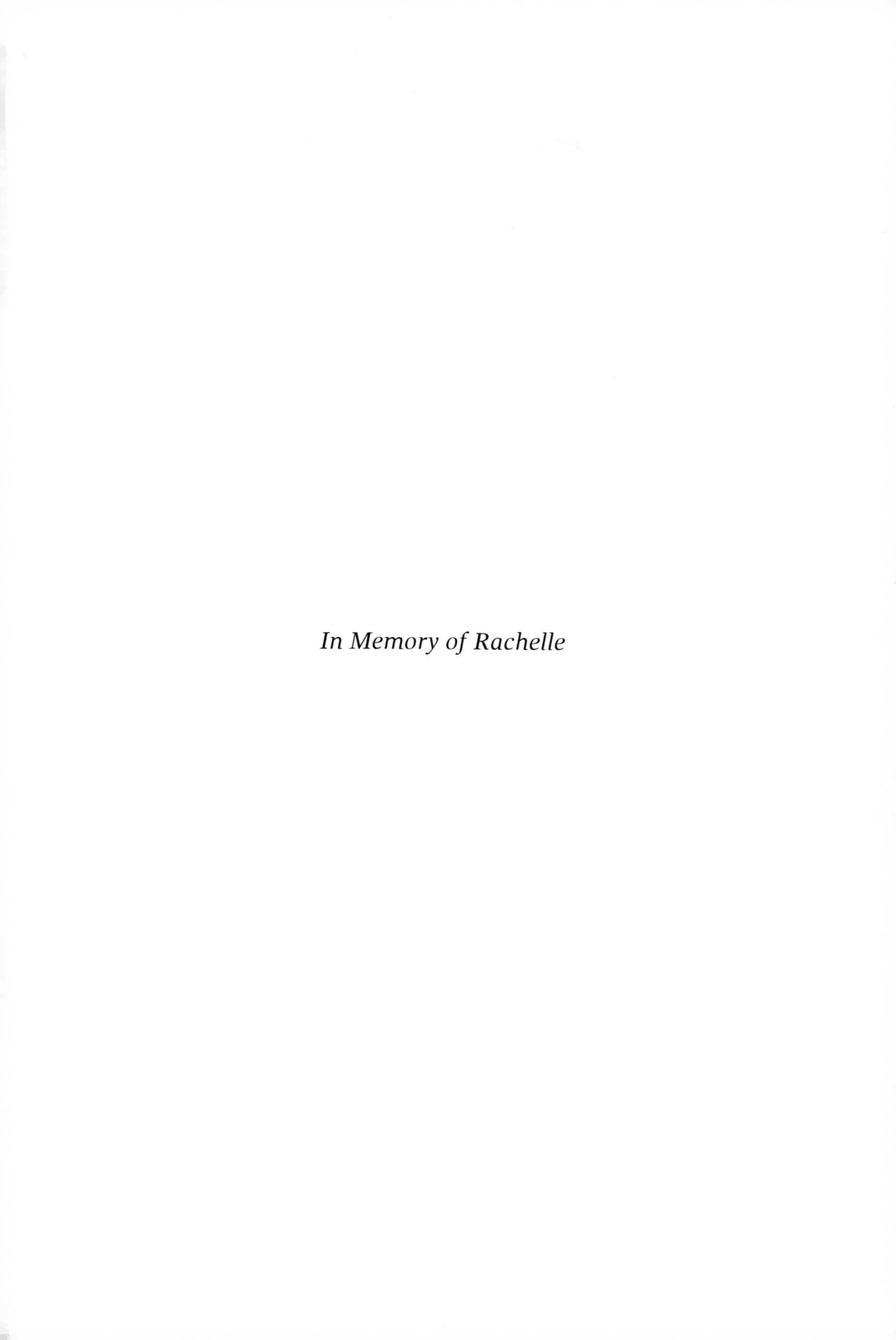

In Memory of Rachelle

Prologue

February 2016

"The road to Bunagana is dangerous," strangers cautioned Argentine and Mapendo. "Some people make it, and some people don't." Argentine and Mapendo tucked their sewing machines into the bottom of woven plastic bags. On top they stuffed a few clothes.

At first light, they set out for the bus station with their families—the adults on crutches, the older children carrying the younger ones on their backs. When they arrived at the bus station, a man piled their possessions onto the roof of a minibus, and they all climbed in. They prayed that this particular minibus, so randomly chosen, would somehow arrive safely on the other side.

"Mungu atusaidie," they whispered. "God help us." Their Swahili was structured like a command to God.

As the minibus pulled onto the bumpy road, Argentine stared at the people filling the roads, remembering her own journey to Goma, atop a truck, years earlier. Now she was headed in the other direction.

Soon the city of Goma faded into the distance, and the road emptied out. The minibus plunged into the heart of the forest with trees crowding the road and blocking the sunlight. Suddenly gunfire punctuated the air.

"Mushuke mbiyo!" the driver whispered to his passengers, his voice tight and tense. "Get down quickly!" One of the passengers threw the door open. The other passengers slid silently off their seats and out of the minibus. They ducked low and sprinted into the trees to hide in the forest, while the sound of gunfire continued up ahead.

Argentine, Mapendo, and Mapendo's husband Joseph, along with all of their children, remained frozen in place on the plastic seats of the minibus. Mapendo clutched her sons to her chest and stared out the window as the other passengers disappeared between the trees. In a few minutes, the minibus had nearly emptied out, and now they were the only passengers remaining. The driver looked at Argentine, Mapendo, and Joseph with their metal leg braces. He saw the crutches propped at their sides, and he shook his head, knowing that for these passengers, with their disabilities, there was no way to run from danger.

"Don't be afraid," the driver whispered in Swahili, then he twisted in his seat and began to reverse the minibus down the road as quietly as possible. After a few minutes, he stopped the minibus again, hoping that he had put enough space between the vehicle and whatever attack was occurring up ahead. He opened his door. "I'll come back," he promised. Then the driver disappeared into the trees to hide.

Argentine, Mapendo, and their families didn't move. They sat there on that lonely stretch of road, in a minibus that everyone else had abandoned.

If the men with guns come, I will beg for mercy, Argentine thought to herself. Then she remembered the money pressed against her skin. *I'll give them everything I have,* she promised herself.

Time passed. It felt like hours. They sat in silence.

Then, suddenly, the driver of the minibus reappeared out of the forest. "Tuende mbiyo." "Let's go quickly," he said as he pulled himself into the front seat. The minibus roared around the bend, then stopped again.

Like magic, the other passengers took shape out of the forest and hoisted themselves back into the bus. The driver floored the gas pedal, and they lurched over bumps, sailed over potholes, and sped off towards Bunagana in a race against the darkening forest.

By the time they arrived in Bunagana it was dark, and fear crackled through the air. As the driver helped Argentine and Mapendo down from the minibus, he looked at them carefully.

"Go and find a place to stay. Lock the door to your room. If anyone comes to the door, don't let them in, no matter what they say," the driver instructed.

The families rented three rooms at a local guest house. They locked the doors, and, in the darkness of those rooms, they collapsed onto the beds.

I didn't hear from Argentine and Mapendo that night. It wasn't until the next day that Mapendo was able to send me a message. "Dada..." she typed on her phone. "Sister...we crossed the border today."

Her message arrived on my phone in the darkness that comes before morning. I woke to the sound of a text message and glanced first at my two-year-old daughter, sleeping beside me. Instinctively I watched the rise and fall of her tiny chest. Then I read the message. "Tumevuka frontière leo." "We crossed the border today."

I sighed in relief. Then I offered up a prayer for whatever part of the journey still lay ahead. None of us could really have imagined the long journey ahead, all they would lose, and all they would gain. But then again, none of us could have imagined everything that led up to this moment.

For me, my part in this journey began in 2006, the year I first moved to Goma, a city in the Democratic Republic of Congo—the city where I would eventually meet Argentine and Mapendo. I found myself moving to eastern Congo because my husband had been offered a job there. I was excited and nervous. I imagined that moving to Congo might offer me the opportunity to live more in touch with the realities that most of the people on our planet face.

The truth is that in Goma I ran headlong into a city where the line between poverty and privilege was hard to escape. I found myself living in a comfortable house next to a family with no house at all. And I found myself trying to build a partnership with Argentine and Mapendo, whose lives existed in a space that I had yet to imagine.

This is the story of all three of our lives, and of who we became—in the place between our fears.

Part I

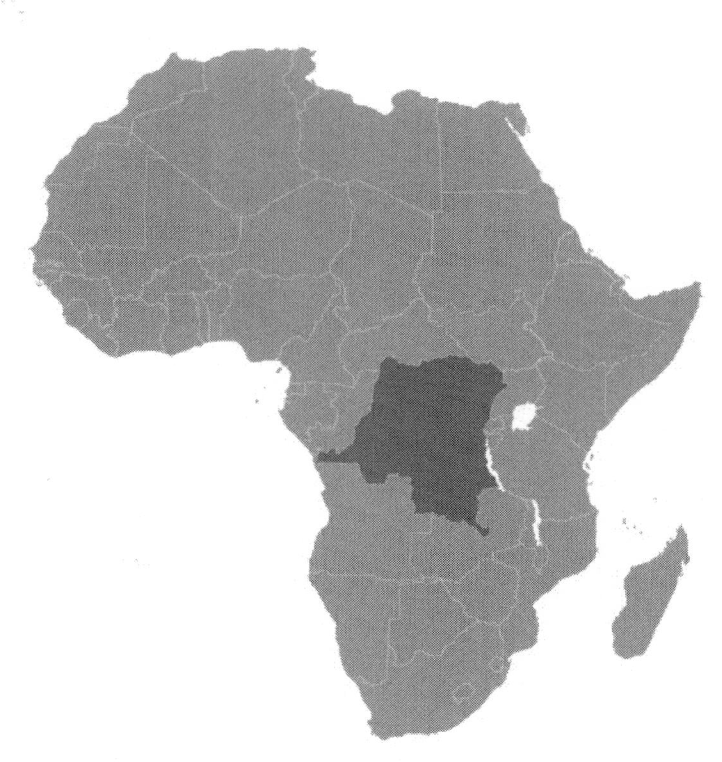

CHAPTER ONE

Fear

July 2006

Tucked in my bed in New York City, I startled awake with visions of a white cloud of gas enveloping an entire city. The countdown had begun. My husband and I were packing up our apartment in the Bronx, gradually leaving more and more furniture on the curb, preparing to move to eastern Congo. We were moving because my husband had a job with a non-profit organization in the city of Goma. My husband had grown up in East Africa and was anxious to return to a region that he loved.

At night before going to bed, I huddled next to my computer pouring over pictures of the city of Goma, trying to imagine my place within it. I remember photos of men hammering metal by the side of the road and women selling beans at the market. In the corners of those photos I found the tell-tale signs of a society on the edge of war. In the shadows of one photo, slouched two young men, rifles slung across their backs. In another photo, I spotted a pick-up truck rigged with machine guns.

But the images of war didn't haunt me at night. I was more afraid of natural disaster.

The city of Goma is caught in the space between Mount Nyiragongo and Lake Kivu. I looked at the photos of Mount

Nyiragongo, an active volcano, puffing smoke during the day and glowing red in the night. *What if the volcano erupted and covered the city with lava?* I knew that was exactly what had happened only four years earlier.

In search of good news, I typed *Lake Kivu* into Google hoping for pictures of a quiet beach. Instead I found an article titled "The Killer Lake."

Clicking on the link, I learned about the large quantities of carbon dioxide and methane gas trapped under heavy pressure at the bottom of Lake Kivu, the result of volcanic activity. My eyes grew wide as I discovered that scientists feared another eruption of Mount Nyiragongo could trigger the lake to explode, releasing a white cloud of poisonous gas that would asphyxiate the entire population along its shores.

My computer screen flashed white as I clicked away from the article. I returned to pictures of women washing clothes at the shore of Lake Kivu. I promised myself that life in Goma would be just fine. *More than half a million people live in Goma,* I told myself. *It can't be that dangerous.*

CHAPTER TWO

All That We Love

The following week, I stood in the airport clutching my phone. I called my parents. "We're leaving now. I love you," I whispered through the air.

"Wait, wait, I'll put you on speaker," my father said.

There was a pause, and then rustling. Finally I could hear both my parents' voices on the other end of the line.

"We're leaving now. I love you," I repeated, unable to find anything else to say.

"I love you too," my mother said.

"Call us when you get there," my father said.

I knew he would be tracking our flight, staring at the computer screen late into the night, waiting for news that my husband and I had arrived safely on the other side.

"Talk to you soon," I promised, and then I hung up. I grabbed my husband's hand. The world was growing too big with the people I loved too far apart. If only I could live in a world where all that I loved stayed in one place.

But the world kept moving. I kept moving. We climbed on the plane, and I studied the beautifully arranged faces of the flight attendants. Their stately expressions soothed the knot in my own stomach. After we took off, I stared out the window, pressing my forehead to the glass, searching for something familiar. But, before I knew it, the world had already disappeared, and there were only clouds below us.

In Europe we switched onto a smaller plane. After a few hours on that plane, I could see the desert below us, and a river snaking through the sand. And then that world also disappeared.

After seven hours in that plane, we began to tilt downward. The captain announced that we were starting our descent toward Kigali, Rwanda and suddenly the world miraculously reappeared below us with soft green hills and shiny tin roofs.

The descent into Kigali was familiar to me. I had first arrived in this airport five years earlier. At that time, my husband and I were newlyweds, and it was my first trip to Africa. I had been excited to see Kigali, the city where my husband grew up. For that trip, my husband's parents met us at the airport. They were still living in Kigali at the time, completing their fortieth year as missionaries in Rwanda and Burundi.

On that first trip I wore a long khaki skirt. When we left the airport and walked toward the car, warm air rushed into my face. My mother-in-law pointed at the red dust swirling around us. "That skirt is going to last about two minutes here," she said with a smile. She had been right.

Now we were approaching Kigali five years later. This time my husband's parents would not be there to greet us at the airport. This was a different type of journey; one that we would make on our own. We would stay in a hotel in Kigali for the night, and then in the morning we would push on to the border of Congo—a border I had never crossed.

As the plane landed, I wiped my hands on my faded jeans and prepared to disembark. The door of the plane opened, and warm air rushed in. The dust of the red earth and the smell of cooking fires welcomed us back.

That night we stayed in a hotel in Kigali. We awoke to the sound of birds outside our windows and ate breakfast on the patio. Then we loaded into a car and drove over green terraced hills toward the Congolese border.

After a few hours, the road curved downward, and I spotted the blue water of Lake Kivu shimmering in the distance. I couldn't see it yet, but I knew that somewhere along the lake was the border to Congo. I grabbed my passport and thumbed through it nervously, quietly wondering why I had never crossed this border before.

CHAPTER THREE

The Border

When we crossed the border into Congo, we entered a different world. The orderly villages of Rwanda faded away. Plastic bags suddenly littered the streets and pumping music spilled from wooden storefronts. There was a pulse to the place.

Money changers nodded their heads in welcome. Motorcycle taxis surged toward us, with the young men racing to see who would arrive first. Above the music, everyone was laughing and shouting.

I loved it immediately.

CHAPTER FOUR

A Place to Live

I loved the hustle of downtown Goma, but my husband and I were immediately whisked away by his colleagues and taken to stay at Hotel Karibu, a beautiful hotel on the outskirts of town. The place was eerily quiet, with hardly any other guests. It was like living in a paradise built at the edge of the world. I wandered the manicured grounds, sat on rocks overlooking Lake Kivu, memorized words in Swahili, and waited for an opportunity to use them.

"Jambo, habari gani?" I would say to the hotel staff, practicing a standard Swahili greeting that I had just learned from an instruction book. After a week in Congo, I had already given up on trying to learn French, frustrated with word endings that trailed off, and vowel combinations that I never got right. Instead, I worked on Swahili, the street language of Goma. I had quickly learned that the woman at the front desk of the hotel spoke in elegant French phrases, but everything she told me was bland and proper. If I wanted to understand the spirit of Goma, the laughter and shouting that I had first heard at the border, I would need Swahili.

A few weeks after we arrived, a middle-aged man who called himself a *commissionaire* took me to look at houses for rent in

Goma. The first thing I noticed was the lava rock walls surrounding every house. Each wall was topped with incredibly beautiful cascades of pink and purple bougainvillea. The flowers looked whimsical, and I imagined the walls were part of an enchanted garden. It was only later that I noticed the glinting spirals of metal beneath the cascades of flowers, razor wire hidden under the blooms.

We arrived at the first house, which was on a green patch of earth near the center of town. I looked at the relatively modest house approvingly. We entered through the kitchen, which featured empty shelves and a long countertop. Then we pushed through a swinging door to the living room, and I jumped back in surprise. A group of men kneeled together in one corner of the bare room. On the grey cement floor was a rag, red with blood. In the center of the gathering, a man held a little boy's arm. Another man held a needle and thread. The man with the needle looked up from the floor, surprised to be interrupted. It seemed we had stumbled into an ad hoc hospital. The commissionaire and I walked quietly back out the kitchen door, with the commissionaire shaking his head. His tour was not starting as planned.

From that green patch of earth, we crossed onto lava rock, looking for the next rental house to visit. Turning my head northward, I could see Mount Nyiragongo ten kilometers (six miles) away in the distance, a plume of smoke puffing from the top.

In Goma the volcano felt ever present but also surprisingly far away, like its smoke would never reach us. I could understand why, during the last eruption in 2002, the population of Goma had watched like spectators as rivers of lava began to thread their way down the mountain in the distance. It wasn't until hours later that panic had suddenly seized the population of Goma. A fissure opened just outside of the city, and it became clear that a river of lava, up to two meters (roughly 6 feet) high, was headed straight for the heart of Goma. Homes and businesses began to vanish under lava. Cars burst into flames, and houses caught fire. The sky grew dark, and the air filled with dust and ash. Chaos swept over the population. Parents grabbed their children and fled over the border to Rwanda. Hospitals emptied out. More than 300,000 people fled the city that day, two thirds of the population at that time. When the population of Goma returned days later, over 120,000 families had lost their homes. The airport runway had been cut in half by a stream of lava, and the business center of Goma had simply disappeared.

Now, only a few years later, large sections of the city remained covered in hardened lava rock. Some neighborhoods were devoid of all vegetation, but I could still feel their pulse. Families had returned to rebuild wooden shacks directly on top of the lava rock, and children played outside, kicking homemade soccer balls on the places where green grass had once grown.

The commissionaire and I were walking through one of these neighborhoods, picking our way over hardened lava rock. The lava stretched several hundred meters (the length of two football fields), and our progress was slow along the uneven surface. It felt like we were walking through a desert, with not a tree in sight, the usually mild sun beating down hard against the rock. We passed by a rusted metal skeleton of a car, forever trapped in the hardened effluent. Little boys began to follow alongside us, and others called out from the side of the road.

And then suddenly we arrived. The commissionaire banged on a red metal gate and a guard opened it, revealing a tall, pointy house crammed into the walled-off property.

When we walked inside the house, I wasn't sure quite what to make of the place. There was no glass in the windows, just holes in the wall, in the whimsical shapes of circles and diamonds. The kitchen had no sink. On the second floor was a winding staircase which led to nowhere. It was a house full of lofty dreams, all of them half-realized.

Soon I discovered that many of these larger houses in Goma had this unfinished air. Many had been built hurriedly over the previous couple of years in response to the exploding population of Goma and the increasing numbers of non-profit organizations using Goma as a base for their work in the region.

In fact, the population of Goma had nearly doubled since the volcanic eruption four years before. Many of the new occupants of Goma were poor villagers seeking refuge from the escalating violence in the surrounding countryside. Tiny wooden shacks, renting for $15 or $20 per month, had multiplied throughout the city, pushing the edges outward.

The increasing insecurity of the region had also drawn international aid and development organizations, like the one my husband was working for. Often those organizations had sizable budgets. I stood staring at the pointed ceiling of this half-finished house, and I realized that my commissionaire was hoping that I had exactly that type of budget.

"If you rent this house, the owner will put glass in the windows. Just imagine a door here, and a closet there. It will be a very good house!" the commissionaire promised confidently. But I wasn't thinking about woodwork or window frames. I just couldn't imagine living in a tall, pointy house that seemed to tower over the wooden shacks just next door.

We didn't find a house to rent that day. But a few weeks later, my husband and I chose a comfortable one-story house in a quiet section of town. We agreed to share it with another American couple who were in Congo volunteering for the year. We split the rent of $600 and moved into that low-slung house with sparkling white-tile floors. In many ways, it was the nicest house I have ever lived in, with two spare guest rooms.

It was also the only house I have ever lived in with a lake view. Soon after we moved in, I discovered that if I stood on my tiptoes at the kitchen window and I looked past the razor wire on our wall, I could see the tiniest sliver of Lake Kivu shimmering in the distance.

CHAPTER FIVE

Mama Kavira

One day, I was washing my dishes and looking out the kitchen window when two women caught my eye. They were walking down our quiet side-street, their forms moving slowly in dusty flip-flops. One of the women was hunched over, her movements deliberate, weighed down by the years. The other form appeared to be a younger woman perhaps in her twenties. Together they looked like mother and daughter. Both women were carrying children on their backs, but my eyes were trained on their heads. While the rest of their bodies swayed, their heads remained immobile, frozen mid-air, their chins jutting outward. I squinted my eyes harder, trying to see what they were carrying on their heads. Finally, I realized they were carrying lava rocks balanced carefully on the crowns of their heads. And I realized they were my neighbors.

These two women, Mama Kavira and Fabiola, lived a few houses down from us. I knew their faces because they lived without a wall. Actually, they lived without a house. They seemed to be squatters on a parcel of land, living in the shadow of a half-built house amidst grey rubble. In one corner of the property, they had fashioned a tiny lean-to shack where they slept, three generations inside at night, lying side by side on a mattress. They lived their lives outside, gathering rocks like furniture around a fire pit. There were white plastic chairs strewn about, and cooking pots stacked on the rocks. There was no outhouse, no electricity, and no water, but, somehow, they arranged their lives.

In retrospect I realize that they probably were not squatting at all. They probably had the landlord's permission to be there, keeping an eye on the property. What I saw as rubble was still a resource to this family, one they had probably worked hard to negotiate, promising the property owner that they would keep an eye on his half-built house.

The older woman, Mama Kavira, often sat with her grown daughters in their outdoor home, laughing and gossiping and calling out to the people passing by on the street. Mama Kavira's grandchildren ran about in torn t-shirts. One of the grandchildren had a physical disability. He was five or six years old with tiny limbs and a head that tilted sideways as though his neck was unable to support it.

Every day, as I walked down the street to the market, I tried to figure out the most polite way to pass by my neighbors in their outside living room. I looked away, imagining I was granting them some form of privacy. But they appeared uninterested in my offers of privacy. As I walked by, they would call out to me in Swahili, "mzungu, mzungu"—"white person, white person." When I finally looked up they would flash a grin and say, "What are you buying for us at the market today?"

I would smile half-heartedly then grit my teeth, already tired of being called mzungu.

On my return from the market, Mama Kavira would call out to me again in that same sing-song voice. "Mzungu, did you buy bread for me at the market today?"

It was a joke, of sorts, I thought. But I was unsure of how to respond, especially in a language I could barely understand. And the laughter of the crowd made me nervous.

There was always a crowd at their makeshift living room. Fabiola braided hair. As I walked by, I would sometimes glance at her customers perched on rocks to have their hair braided. I envied those Congolese women with their casual conversations and easy laughter.

One day I decided to get the upper hand of their ongoing joke. I bought an extra loaf of bread at the market and contemplated the best way to present it. I thought it would be best to walk casually by, eyes cast downward as usual. When the question came, I would reach into my bag and brandish the long loaf of bread like a sword.

On this day the sky was blue. The sun shone high in the sky as I made my way home from the market. I began to pass my neighbors, and I realized the group was caught in a conversation. *Perhaps they won't notice me today,* I thought, vaguely disappointed. Then a voice rang out.

"Mzungu, mzungu, did you buy bread for me at the market today?" Mama Kavira called out to me.

I stopped in the middle of the tree-lined road and reached into my bag. The crowd focused their eyes on me, and the suspense began to build. In that moment I saw my mistake. The bread had fallen to the bottom of the large bag, and now I couldn't find it. I was stuck in the middle of the road, searching through my green plastic bag like it was a magic box of tricks. The crowd's fascination grew. I shuffled through a canister of hot chocolate, tea bags, a jar of peanut butter, and a prized acquisition of Quaker Oats. This was taking far too long. Finally, I located the loaf of bread at the bottom of my bag, now oddly misshapen. Triumphantly, I whipped the loaf of bread out of the plastic bag.

"Mkati," I declared. It was one of my new words in Swahili. "Bread."

Mama Kavira reached out and took the bread. The crowd howled with laughter, louder than I had ever heard them before.

"Mkati, mkati! Mzungu alituletea mkati!" they exclaimed in amusement. "Bread, Bread! The white person brought us bread!"

The laughter stung my ears, and I hurried home.

I began to search for an alternate route to the market. Surely there had to be some other path to the main road. But our little road was itself half-built, it slanted down and then disappeared altogether. There was only one way out. Each day I took a deep breath and continued to walk by my neighbors, struggling to find a carefree expression to wear on my face.

One day, shortly after the bread incident, I was passing by Mama Kavira when I noticed she was beckoning me toward her. "Mzungu, mzungu," she called out. I froze, and then decided that I had nothing left to lose. I picked my way through the rubble, and to my surprise the older woman gestured toward a rock, offering me a seat. "Karibu," she said to me. Karibu is perhaps the one Swahili word that every visitor to Goma knows. It means welcome, and it is offered to almost everyone on nearly all occasions.

"Starehe," I replied, giving a standard response. Laughter ripped through the crowd, my one-word answer causing an unreasonable amount of excitement. The crowd's laughter threw me off again. I wondered if I had gotten the word wrong.

Embarrassed, I cast my eyes down, staring at the rubble on the ground. The seconds ticked by. Eventually, there was no place to look but up.

My eyes rose to Mama Kavira's face, lined by the years, shining with amusement. For the first time I began to imagine that she wasn't trying to be unkind.

Slowly I let go of my pride and my embarrassment. I settled into my place on that rock. Then I took a deep breath, leaned my head back, and began to laugh.

CHAPTER SIX

Rocks

Eventually, I gathered enough words in Swahili to ask Mama Kavira and her daughter, Fabiola, why they had been carrying lava rocks on their heads that day.

"Where were you going?" I asked.

Mama Kavira rubbed her thumb and forefinger together.

"Makuta," she said. "Money."

I must have looked confused because she stood up and motioned for me to follow her.

We walked down the street, our forms bent together, as I tried to follow the Swahili conversation.

After a few minutes, Mama Kavira stopped in the middle of the road and turned toward a lava rock wall that circled a half-built house. We stared at the wall together. Mama Kavira touched a finger to the rock, then she lifted her hand to her head, as though carrying something.

"Majiwe. Makuta." "Rocks. Money."

I looked at Mama Kavira, picturing how she had carried her grandson on her back and those rocks on her head, working day after day, to build someone else's wall. I wondered how much money she might have earned from her labor. Clearly, whatever she had earned it was not enough to afford a roof over her own head—never mind a wall.

CHAPTER SEVEN

McMansions

While the blatant disparities in Goma haunted me, they also pulled me in. They testified to a reality I had always known existed...the poor carried rocks on their heads to build the walls of the wealthy while giant SUVs with tinted windows rumbled past men pushing wooden carts. Children carried yellow containers of water on their heads while people like me swam in the sparkling blue pool at Hotel Karibu.

I knew that in the United States the reality was not so very different; the disparities were just better hidden. In the US, zoning laws, school district boundaries, and a long history of redlining had all worked to create communities where we tended to live next to people with similar resources. But I knew other realities existed.

In New York, I taught in a public high school in the South Bronx. The school was located less than ten miles from the fortunes of Wall Street, but photocopies were a limited resource doled out like gold. The first year at my school, when I asked my supervisor what book I should teach to my ninth-grade students, she took me to the closet which doubled as the English department's bookroom. She told me to try and choose a title where we had at least thirty-four copies, a full classroom set, so my students wouldn't need to share during class. "Make sure no one takes the books home, or you won't have enough for your other class," she had said. *But how will my students ever read a novel, if they can't take it home,* I had wondered.

In Goma, the disparities were easier to see. Mama Kavira lived right outside my door. Walking by her poverty made my comparative wealth feel ridiculous and uncomfortable. It didn't matter that in the United States I had never been anything other than middle class. Or that in Congo I had tried to choose a relatively modest house. The truth was that in Goma I lived with white tile floors and a red tin roof. Mama Kavira and her children lived with lava rock under their feet, and all day long their roof was the sky.

CHAPTER EIGHT

Sewing

Every day that I walked down the street, I waved at Mama Kavira. "Habari, Mama?" I would greet her, practicing my Swahili.

She always responded cheerfully but, out of the corner of my eye, I saw the white plastic chairs with no table, the children who never went to school, the little boy with his head tilting sideways...it all distilled into a single point. *These* were my neighbors, and every day that I walked down the street, I was passing them by.

Looking for something concrete to do, I bought a hand-crank sewing machine and proposed to Mama Kavira that she and I could learn to sew. She laughed, saying she was too old to learn to sew, then pointed at her daughter Fabiola. Fabiola agreed instantly.

Mama Kavira and Fabiola started coming to my house in the afternoons. We put the sewing machine on my dining-room table and stared at it. None of us knew how to thread the machine. We wrapped brightly colored thread around knobs and levers in various configurations, hoping to stumble on success. The first dozen times, the thread broke as soon as we turned the wheel. Eventually it began to pull forward, producing a whirring sound and neat little stitches on top of the cloth. We were thrilled, until we flipped the cloth over to discover a mess of knotted-up thread underneath.

Eventually we figured out how to adjust the tension, and our stitches began to come out reasonably well, on top and underneath. While Fabiola and I practiced sewing, Mama Kavira paced back and forth in our living room, wearing her one-year-old grandson on her back, soothing him to sleep. Diane, Fabiola's three-year-old daughter, played on our furniture, eventually abandoning herself to a nap. She had no diapers and often peed on the cushions of our couch in her sleep.

"Hakuna shida!" "Don't worry!" I would say. "I love children...I love having you here...I love pee on my furniture!" I proclaimed, getting carried away by my own enthusiasm.

But it was true. I was happy to have them there. They were the first friends I made in Congo.

CHAPTER NINE

At Every Corner

When I wasn't sewing, I layered on sunscreen and headed out to the main road, hoping to explore Goma and practice my Swahili. I would often head to Yesu Ni Jibu (Jesus is The Answer) a small shop on the main road that had miraculously cornered the market on American comfort food, stocking jars of peanut butter and cans of Pringles arrayed in rainbow colors.

I passed by vendors selling almost everything by the side of the road. In one area there were rows upon rows of high- heeled shoes carefully laid out on a tarp. Every day that I walked by, I stared at the shoes, pointy and glittery, imagining the teenage girl in the United States who might have worn them to the prom before tossing them into a donation bin.

Who wears these shoes in Goma? I asked myself, eyeing my own feet, clad in flip-flops, scuffed from the lava rock. To me, life in Goma did not call for high heels. But I began paying attention to the people walking all around me on the street. To my right, a woman stepped out of a tiny wooden shack looking for all the world as though she had stepped from the pages of a magazine. She was dressed in a brilliantly colored and perfectly fitted African outfit, with off-the-shoulder sleeves and a scalloped neckline. On her feet, glistened pointy high-heeled shoes.

I watched that woman carefully as she made her way down the street, fascinated by the miracle I was witnessing. She held her head high and gently lifted each foot, placing it one step forward, perfectly situated between the garbage and the rubble of Goma. She might have been walking down a runway at a Paris fashion show.

I followed that regal woman down the street that day, waiting to see where she was headed, imagining some grand party, perhaps at one of the fancy hotels. But then she turned in at a nondescript shop, and I was left staring after her. Soon, I noticed another woman, similarly dressed, with high-heeled shoes, and I walked alongside her. She turned in at the hospital. Another woman paraded by, then turned in at the market. Eventually I realized that these impeccably dressed women were going everywhere, or nowhere in particular. They were simply the women of Congo, a place that celebrates style, color and beauty in the face of every obstacle.

CHAPTER TEN

Farther Down the Road

Walking farther down the road, I stumbled on the rest of life. Older women sat by the side of the road with vats of oil balanced over charcoal fires. Younger girls sat at wooden crates, selling salt, sugar and palm oil in plastic sandwich bags, just enough for one day's use—poverty tackled by portion size.

The streets of Goma always felt like a party to me; a party in a fascinating language I couldn't quite understand. People stopped in the middle of the road to greet one another in Swahili, French, or sometimes other languages. There are 242 languages spoken in Congo. While French is the official language, Lingala, Kituba, Swahili and Tshiluba are all designated as national languages as well. In Goma, almost everyone spoke Swahili. People with high school educations also spoke French. Very few people spoke English. I loved that. It forced me to swim through Swahili and try to absorb it. Or, sometimes I simply surrendered myself to the music that blared from every tiny wooden shop. On one corner, I would hear the smooth beats of the latest American pop-song, and on the next corner I would hear the fast and unforgettable rhythms of Congolese music.

The streets of Goma also featured food. Girls walked by with large platters of yellow bananas on their heads. Little boys sold peanuts, freshly roasted, salted, and sealed into little plastic bags. Other boys carried basins of soda bottles, clanking the bottle opener against the glass of the soda bottles, calling out to customers. For 200 francs, they would hand over a soda, open it for me, and collect the bottle at the end of my drink.

One day, as I was exploring, I noticed a row of beach umbrellas lined up in the dirt off one side of the road. My brain registered the colorful umbrellas, the dirt, the sun beating down, and the crowds of people. *Ice cream carts*, I thought hopefully.

But what I found were photocopy machines, beige and blocky, sitting in the dirt under the beach umbrellas. I had only ever seen such machines tucked into the corners of offices. Now here they were in the dirt, whirring away under beach umbrellas, extension cords leading into a building nearby. Students from the nearby university queued up to photocopy course material in the sun. When the electricity cut off, the photocopy vendors fired up their own generators.

In a city with many students, very few textbooks, and only occasional electricity, the people of Goma put photocopiers under beach umbrellas, bought generators, and built a business.

This is what I loved about Goma. Every day I would discover something that I thought I knew, like a photocopy machine, in exactly the place I never expected to find it. I would stare at it for a moment, surprised by the novelty, and then I would think, *Hmm...that is a great idea.*

CHAPTER ELEVEN

Under a Tin Roof

One day, I was on my way home from Yesu Ni Jibu when the sky suddenly grew dark. The vendors began to disappear. By the time I reached the man selling high heels, he was piling the shoes in a bundle on his tarp. The wind was picking up, and I could taste the rain in the air. The doors to the shops began to close, and motorcycle taxis whizzed by. I tried to walk faster, almost running, but then fat drops of rain began to fall, and I was still a long way from home. As I looked up, I realized I was the only person on the road.

"Mzungu, mzungu, unaenda wapi?" I heard people calling out to me from the side of the road. "White person, white person, where are you going?"

Glancing to my side I saw that everyone else had gathered under the awnings of nearby tin roofs. The small patches of protection underneath each awning looked full but I picked one and approached. A barefoot little boy with his shirt faded yellow stood next to a man in a three-piece suit, his shoes polished. A market woman, with a giant bundle of charcoal, had crowded in beside him. She motioned me toward her. "Karibu, mzungu," the market woman said. "Welcome, white person."

I wasn't the only person she was greeting. Under that awning, I looked around and saw that everyone was greeting each other. The man in the three-piece suit was greeting people in French, shaking hands, as though we all had just arrived at a formal event, as though our shirts weren't wet, and our shoes weren't splattered with mud.

Soon, the rain began to pound so hard against the tin roof that our conversations came to a halt. We all stared out at the rain, lost in our own thoughts.

Eventually the rain steadied into a slower beat, and people began to chat again. The man with the suit bought peanuts from the boy standing next to him. The market woman sank down beside her bundle and relaxed.

Then the wind picked up again, blowing bits of rain under the roof. Our dry area shrank, and we inched more tightly together, each of us checking the edges of our gathering to make sure that no one was left out in the rain.

"Sogea kidogo." "Move over a little," the market woman said as she tried to make space for the person beside her. For that moment, we were a community.

And then the rain stopped. The little boy ran off first, splashing recklessly in the puddles. The man in the suit wiped away the mud from his shoes and stepped out gingerly, wishing everyone a good afternoon. The market woman slowly stretched her arms to the sky and piled the bundle back on her head. I stepped into the sun and disappeared into the crowd.

A day or two later, I passed by a man I remembered from the awning. "Jambo," he greeted me. "Jambo sana," I responded as I walked by, and then we both smiled just a little, remembering that small piece of life we had shared.

CHAPTER TWELVE

The Guard Shack

Our house came with a guard shack. We had an alternating assortment of guards who sat in it, choosing to earn extra income after their regular shifts at my husband's office. The guards greeted me, opening and closing the metal gate as I headed out to explore Goma. They endured my endless attempts at Swahili, even though they would rather converse in the English they were working so hard to learn. They would nod approvingly when my husband occasionally brought home one of the white SUVs from work, and they would raise their eyebrows suspiciously when Fabiola and her children arrived barefoot.

I hated the guard shack and everything it stood for. But I believed what I was told.

"It isn't safe to live without a guard."

"You, as a foreigner, are a natural target..."

It was true that Goma was unsafe at night. The city lived in a form of self-imposed lock-down from dusk until dawn. At night, armed men broke into houses, demanding cash. There was no 911, no public emergency number, to call. For the wealthy, there were a few security services that could be hired. They sent out a truck with men with guns if there was an emergency in the middle of the night. *Sometimes* the truck arrived in time.

For the rest of the population, the vast majority living in small wooden structures with no razor wire and no guard outside, poverty offered little relief from the violence. Families with no electricity or running water, with plastic sheeting covering their walls and floors of lava rock, invested first in double locks for the door. Yet it seemed the wooden doors could always be knocked down and the wooden shutters on their windows forced open. Families waited in silence through the night, often unable to sleep, listening for thieves at the door or window.

When a family heard attackers at their doors or their windows, they relied on the only weapon in their possession—their voices. They shouted, "Tuko macho! Tuko macho!"—"We are awake! We are awake!" in hopes of scaring the attackers away. If the neighbors heard their shouts they too would pound on their walls and shout, "Tuko macho! Tuko macho!" until the whole cluster of houses was alive with the sounds of people calling out to each other.

The danger in Goma was real. And it seemed to have little to do with an exploding lake, which, to be honest, I had not thought about very often since I arrived. Still, this other kind of danger was always in the air. It kept the streets empty at night. And sometimes, even during the day, rumors of gunfire would cause the streets to suddenly empty out. But most of the time, life in Goma felt bright and full of energy. And as I passed through our metal gate on my way to the market, I often wished we didn't have a guard at our gate.

I was told that it was customary to bring a plate of food out to the guard at dinnertime. To me it seemed rude to leave the guard eating in that small shack, so I began inviting the guards inside for dinner. We ate together at our long wooden table, often with the other American couple with whom we shared the house.

"Soooo...how was your day?" I would ask in tentative Swahili. Some of the guards played along, happily launching into discussions of the latest news. One of the guards was a part-time pastor and would relish the opportunity to offer religious instruction as we ate our meal. But other guards appeared unsure about their presence at our dining room table, or perhaps it was just my conversational strategies that threw them off. One guard, named Dieu Donné, would smile sheepishly but remain silent, as though unsure how to respond. I wondered if perhaps he had preferred eating his dinner in the guard shack, his portable radio filling the silence. Or perhaps the silence was only awkward to me, with my American affinity for dinnertime conversation. Later, one of my friends told me that she thought it was rude to talk while eating. "We like to concentrate on eating," she explained.

CHAPTER THIRTEEN

The Market

Finally, after a few months in Goma, I decided it was time to try my hand at the market. I prepared a list of things to buy—tomatoes and onions, supplies for dinner that night.

"I am going to the market," I said, waving goodbye to a Congolese friend who lived nearby. I was wearing a small cloth purse slung across my chest.

"Oh no!" My friend piped up in surprise. "That purse will never do. The thieves can cut off a cloth strap."

I imagined dangerous-looking men wielding scissors.

My friend disappeared into her house and reemerged carrying a large purse like one my grandma might have carried, with sturdy handles and fake alligator skin. "Here. Carry a purse like this," she said. This new purse seemed like a worse idea to me, easily torn from my grip. But, come to think of it, I did recall seeing Congolese women carrying hefty purses like this. Walking down the streets, I had noticed the strange contrast between their beautiful African outfits and the fake leather purses. I had also noticed that the Congolese women had often abandoned the handles of their purses altogether. Instead they would carry these purses balanced on top of their heads, just as Mama Kavira had carried the lava rock.

I declined the fake alligator skin purse my friend offered me and settled instead on tucking cash in the front pocket of my jeans. My friend glanced at me, then shook her head, appalled by my strategy.

When I arrived at the market, I was greeted by a group of small boys. They saw me approach from far away, my pale skin layered in sunscreen. They ran toward me and crushed in on me in complete chaos.

Some of the boys held up small black plastic bags that they sold for fifty francs, and others showed off larger green plastic bags for one hundred francs. All of them were vying for the chance to sell me plastic bags that I could carry into the market.

I tried to shove past the boys, fixing my eyes on the market ahead, and reaching for my own cloth bags, saying, "Niko na sac"—"I have a bag."

This approach was an unmitigated disaster. The crowd of boys followed me through one section of the market after another. They grabbed at my arm in indignation, shoved plastic bags in my face, and caused such a ruckus that it felt like the entire market was watching me.

Finally, I halted my forward march and turned around, letting my eyes settle on one boy, the closest one toward me. He was still holding up his green plastic bags proudly.

Our eyes locked. "Cent francs," he said. It was the equivalent of twenty cents.

"Nipe tatu." "Give me three," I replied in resignation.

The boy ripped the bags off the stack, and I handed over the three hundred francs. The other boys fell back immediately. I breathed.

But as I started to make my way forward again, I noticed that my plastic bag vendor was quietly shadowing me. I turned left down one aisle. Then I turned right down another aisle. He was still there. I decided to ignore him. But when I paused to buy some tomatoes, arranged in pyramids on the table, the boy rushed to my side. I reached to open the green plastic bag he had sold me, and he snatched it out of my hands, flinging it open with a flourish.

Without even looking at me, the tomato vendor, who had already taken my money, nodded at the boy and murmured something. She placed my bright red tomatoes carefully in the boy's outstretched green plastic bag.

Flummoxed, I marched on. For each item I bought, the boy held out his bag.

By the end of our tour, the boy was carrying all three bags weighed down by beans, tomatoes, bananas, onions, and peas. I was beginning to wonder how I would ever get my bags back from him.

Perhaps it would have been better to have encountered those scissors-wielding thieves than this little boy who won't leave me alone, I thought to myself.

Finally, we reached the market exit, and to my utter astonishment, the little boy handed the bags back to me. "Asante sana." "Thank you very much," I said. He looked at me. I reached in my front pocket and pulled out another one hundred francs.

The little boy took the crumpled bill and smiled happily. Then he pointed over to the motorcycle taxis and I nodded in agreement. As he ran off to arrange a ride for me, I stood there holding the bags, feeling their heaviness for the first time...tomatoes, bananas, beans, onions, peas...

I had been overwhelmed by the group of boys and so caught up in my determination not to get ripped off that I had failed to see what was right before me, a little boy carrying my bags for me. In the United States, he might have been in third or fourth grade. Here he was selling plastic bags.

The boy returned with a motorcycle taxi, skidding to a stop in front of me. I climbed on the motorcycle, balancing the green plastic bags in front of me and grabbing the seat behind me to steady myself. And then we were off, the market and Mount Nyiragongo at our backs, the rush of the wind in my ears. As we cruised forward, I closed my eyes and thought of that little boy who had carried my bags. I wished I had asked him his name.

CHAPTER FOURTEEN

Teaching

Eventually, after three or four months, a friend offered me a job teaching English at one of the local universities. I was grateful for the opportunity. Each morning I walked out to the main road, waved at Mama Kavira, and then flagged down a motorcycle taxi which would carry me down the lakeshore road and out to the university at the edge of town.

The first day I arrived at my class, I walked into the large, open air room and was shocked to discover nearly seventy students inside, almost all male. "Good morning," I began, my voice bouncing off the walls. The class immediately fell silent. They opened their notebooks and looked at the blackboard expectantly. In all my years teaching in New York City, I had never heard a classroom fall so silent.

CHAPTER FIFTEEN

Lost Villages

2007

For the remainder of that first year, I taught my classes at the local university and then returned home in the afternoons to continue sewing with Fabiola. Fabiola was the same age as many of my students at the university, but the two worlds couldn't have seemed more different. My students were in the engineering department, with hopes of going on to further studies in Europe or North America. While I talked to those students, I often wondered what kind of homes they had come from, what kind of mixture of hard work and good fortune had framed their lives, that they had made it through fourteen or more years of schooling in a country as unstable as Congo. I knew that most parents in Congo struggled to pay school fees for their children. By the age of ten or eleven, most children's educations had been broken into bits and pieces, scattered somewhere between the months they went to school and the months they couldn't afford to do so.

In the afternoon as we sewed, I would ask Fabiola about her own life, in my uncertain Swahili.

"Did you ever go to school?" I asked.

"I started primary school once..." she replied.

"When did you stop?" I continued.

"I don't even know," Fabiola said, shrugging her shoulders.

Sometimes I would learn other bits of Fabiola's life. I gathered that the family hadn't always lived in Goma, in the rubble of someone else's land. One time, Fabiola told me the name of her village, a place where they once had a home. I wondered where that home had gone.

CHAPTER SIXTEEN

The Apartment

July 2007

When that first year ended, the American couple who we shared the house with returned to the United States. My husband and I began searching for another place to live. The house we lived in was far larger than we needed on our own, and I was growing ever-more frustrated with living behind a lava rock wall, where my friends had to bang on a gate and ask a guard for permission to enter. I wanted to live without a wall.

I fell in love with a simple apartment on the second floor of a large trucking compound in the center of town. The compound still had a wall and a guard, but at least we weren't the only ones inside. In fact, the compound contained what seemed like an entire village inside. Woodworkers pounded out furniture, and boys unloaded trucks. Families lived in various constructions inside the compound. There was a man who ran an embroidery machine and a restaurant inside a trucking container that served plates of beans, rice, and meat. Outside of the container, underneath a tarp, men sat drinking bottles of cold Primus beer.

The apartment offered me a second-floor view of everything that I loved about Congo, the endless energy and hustle, the people living side by side, and the strange juxtapositions of women carrying jugs of water, and planes flying by overhead.

We moved into the apartment, sharing a balcony with a Congolese family next door. The head of the family, Papa Thanks, was the manager of the compound. The women of his family sat on that balcony all day—sorting beans, roasting meat and washing clothes.

Papa Thanks's family was always kind to me. When I walked past them, they smiled and nodded their greetings casually, and then went back to whatever they were doing. They never once addressed me as mzungu, pretending instead that I fit right in. I couldn't have asked for a better gift.

Sometimes in the evening, I sat in the shadow of our doorway, stretching my legs out onto the balcony before me. I would watch the sun set over the trucking compound and offer up a silent prayer of thanks—grateful that, at least for that moment, there was no longer a wall between me and my neighbors.

CHAPTER SEVENTEEN

A Knock

One day, shortly after we moved into the apartment, I heard a knock. I opened the door to find Mama Kavira, Fabiola, and her two children on our balcony. Carrying the children on their backs, they had walked the five kilometers (three miles) from our old neighborhood to our new apartment.

The women on Papa Thanks's balcony greeted Mama Kavira and Fabiola politely, unsure what to make of my visitors with their beaten-down flip-flops and ragged t-shirts.

We shared tea and bread and traded stories from the old neighborhood. The children played on the cement floor. Fabiola wanted to start sewing again.

For several weeks she made the trip daily and our sewing endeavors continued. But one day money went missing from our apartment. It was $200, our rent money for the month. The money had been stashed in my bedroom, in a drawer with my underwear.

I knew that whoever had taken the money needed it more than I did. But still I couldn't stomach the feeling of friends waiting for me to turn my back and then rifling through my underwear drawer.

I asked Fabiola and Mama Kavira if they knew what happened to the money.

"Sikufaa kitu," Fabiola insisted. "I didn't do anything." Then she dropped to her knees and began to wail.

Horrified, I grabbed Fabiola's hands and tried to pull her up, but she stayed planted there. In the stark light of Goma, I could see our figures casting shadows on the wall, one towering over the other.

"Hakuna shida! Hakuna shida!" "No problem! No problem!" I said, still trying to pull her up. She refused to move. Words stuck in my throat and came out hollow.

Now everything had gone doubly wrong, and I longed to return to the original problem. Missing money could have been forgotten, but I would never forget how quickly Fabiola fell to her knees before me. Whatever story of equality I had envisioned for us had melted in an instant, the line between poverty and privilege still stubbornly intact.

I never found out for sure what happened to that money, but that was the last day Fabiola and I sewed together...the work required a level of intimacy we were no longer able to muster. Still Fabiola never disappeared from my life in Goma, and instead we tried other endeavors. I bought charcoal for her to resell and helped her rent a house for a while. But it seemed like everything she tried eventually fell apart under the pressure of too many family needs and too few resources. For Fabiola, life had fallen apart a long time before, and no matter how hard she tried, she couldn't figure out how to put it back together again.

CHAPTER EIGHTEEN

Motards

For my students at the university across town, life seemed to have a more upward trajectory. They worked hard, photocopying their course materials and juggling life.

The only problem with my job was that the commute had gotten significantly longer since we moved across town. My husband bought me a helmet to wear on my motorcycle taxi rides. The helmet was new and flashy and two sizes too big. But still I promised to wear it.

In the mornings I would walk out my door with a backpack on my shoulder and the motorcycle helmet dangling from my fingertips. As soon as I walked out of the trucking compound, a few motorcycle taxi drivers would catch sight of me and come racing toward me.

In Goma, the young men who drive motorcycle taxis are called *motards*, after the French word. Goma is full of motards. They occupy a world unto themselves. They rarely own the motorcycles that they ride, instead they rent them by the week, hoping to save up enough earnings for a different future. My motorcycle drivers often talked of one day buying their own motorcycles, or of opening a shop, or of getting married to a mzungu who would take them to the United States. But saving money in Goma is like saving air, especially for these young men, who lived one accident away from disaster. In the evenings I saw some of them at the bars near our house, arguing and laughing—shrugging off the dust from the roads and drinking their earnings away.

In the mornings the motards were more alert. They gathered at street corners or, if they had enough gas money, they raced around the streets in search of passengers.

"Mzungu, tuende." "White person, let's go," they would offer, as I walked out of the trucking compound.

I would pick one and attempt to negotiate a price. Then I would strap on my helmet and climb on the back of the motorcycle, holding on to the edge of the seat behind me. Off we would race across town, weaving between cars, wooden carts and market women carrying charcoal. We would make our way through the traffic-jammed main road and then race onto the lakefront road toward the outskirts of town. I loved the feeling of weightlessness as we sped out of town and the way I could only hear the rush of the wind in my ears.

But before we could reach the lakefront road, we often found ourselves stuck in traffic on the main road. There were often accidents on that road, and the accidents usually involved motorcycles. I remember passing slowly by accidents and often catching sight of a motorcycle spun off into the dirt. Sometimes, I could see a body sprawled out. Always, there were other motards nearby, throwing rocks or blockading the road in protest at the death or injury of one of their own.

Despite the traffic and accidents in town, finding a motard at the beginning of the day was always easy. Finding a ride home was harder. The university campus was way out past Hotel Karibu where motorcycle taxis were less likely to be passing by when I finished my classes. Often, I would start my way home on foot, my helmet still dangling from my fingertips. This caused no end of amusement to the people walking by. Women walking in the opposite direction, carrying platters of bananas or bundles of charcoal, would break into grins as I approached. "Motard, motard," they called out to me, tongue in cheek, "did you lose your motorcycle?" Then they would break down into laughter. The joke was meant to amuse themselves after a long day.

But I called out in response anyway, "Ndiyo! Nimepoteza kabisa." "Yes! I have lost it for sure."

"Eh! Mzungu anasema Kiswahili!" "The white person speaks Swahili!" they would exclaim, laughing harder. I could never be sure whether they were more amused by my ridiculous helmet or my unexpected attempt at Swahili.

Still, I liked the joke. There was a sense of camaraderie to it. For a moment, we were just regular people walking down the road, all of us wishing for a motard to carry us home.

Finally, though, I grew tired of my unpredictable commute. At the end of the semester, I decided to stop teaching at the university. The motorcycle ride seemed too long and too dangerous, and I felt determined to find some other way to engage with the world. Without realizing it, I was leaving space open for a world I had yet to discover.

CHAPTER NINETEEN

Mzungu

Living in the downtown district of Birere introduced me to a different side of Goma. In the shops near our apartment, I often ran into Indian and South African soldiers shopping for electronics. Standing by the side of the road, I watched convoys of those soldiers with weapons and flak jackets, as they headed out of town to the rural areas surrounding Goma. Their transport trucks were white, with MONUC emblazoned on the side, a French acronym for the United Nations Mission in the Democratic Republic of Congo. My breath would often catch in my throat when I saw their familiar looking pickup trucks with machine guns stationed on back.

At the time the United Nations had 17,000 soldiers stationed throughout eastern Congo. In the late 1990s, the country had been wracked by two successive wars, the First and Second Congo Wars, also known as the First African World War and the Great War of Africa, due to the large number of countries involved in the fighting. The Lusaka Ceasefire Agreement had been signed in 1999, and the UN had sent troops to monitor the ceasefire. Despite the presence of MONUC troops, fighting had continued in eastern Congo as the central government (based in the western part of the country) struggled to maintain control.

Throughout the next decade, rebel groups (often backed by neighboring countries) continued to fight for control of eastern Congo, clashing with local militia and government forces (FARDC). The ongoing fighting brought an enormous influx of arms into the region, ravaged local villages, and exacerbated ethnic tensions. By the time I arrived in Goma, MONUC peace-keepers were stationed throughout the region but the peace felt wobbly at best.

The streets of downtown Birere were narrow, with lava rock strewn about. In the rainy season, rivers of mud poured through the streets, and people hopped from rock to rock, laying out cardboard in the spaces between the rocks like self-made bridges. On the sides of the road were tiny wooden shacks, built nearly on top of each other, like miniature row-houses. Tangles of electric wires snaked from one house to the next, and the flimsy wooden homes often caught on fire. Men pushed giant wooden carts through the streets. Some of these carts were as big as the bed of a pick-up truck. Multiple men would be engaged in the challenge of navigating the cart, sweat glistening on their brows.

One day, I was trekking through the streets of Birere and practicing my Swahili, when I glanced at the setting sun and realized it would be dark soon. At the same time, I realized I had no idea where I was. Usually I kept a pretty good eye on my turns, so I could backtrack as needed. But on this day, I had gotten distracted and wandered into a part of Birere that I didn't recognize at all.

I stood at an intersection, wondering which way might lead me home, peering down one winding road after another without recognizing anything. The streets were packed with people headed home for the night. They circled around me, rushed past me, almost bumped into me.

I was still standing there in the middle of that intersection when a jolt ran through my body. I stumbled forward trying to catch myself from falling. A young man had pushed past me, shoving me hard and mumbling something in Swahili. I didn't catch the words, only the shove and the dismissiveness in his voice, and one word, hanging on the edge of his sentence. "Mzungu," he said.

Perhaps it was because I was lost and scared. Or perhaps I had finally collected enough Swahili words to match my growing indignation at being called "mzungu" every time I walked out my door. As the young man pushed past me, I whipped around and grabbed his arm angrily, pulling him backwards. "I am not a mzungu! I have a name," I shouted.

The crowded street fell suddenly silent in my ears.

The mood in Goma can change in an instant. Angry motards can barricade the street. Crowds can start shouting. In a region where government institutions have failed to protect people, the population has learned to take matters into its own hands. I remembered stories of thieves who had been caught in the street and stoned by enraged crowds.

I stood there in Birere, my own voice echoing in my ears and the darkness falling in upon me.

The young man that I had grabbed stared back at me; his expression unreadable. I let go of his arm. Then he laughed, shrugging his shoulders, my indignation entirely inexplicable to him.

In that moment, I learned what I always should have known. It didn't matter how many streets I walked down, or how many words I proudly collected in my Swahili notebook. I would always be a mzungu—a visitor in this place—in this city that I loved.

CHAPTER TWENTY

Sharing a Plate

September 2007

One day my husband suggested to me that I should visit the Centre pour Handicapés. "I met this woman who has a sewing group there. I think you would like her," he said. I had never been to the Center, but I knew it was a Catholic project in the heart of Goma, near the cathedral. The cathedral was unforgettable. In 2002 it had stood directly in the path of the lava flow. Molten lava raced through the building and melted away the roof, leaving a single, giant stone wall standing above the rubble, shaped like a triangle. Every time I went to Virunga market, I passed by the cathedral, standing there as both a memorial to the Goma that had melted away in 2002 and as a testament to all that remained standing. Briefly I wondered if the Center had been in the path of the lava as well, and what that would have meant for the people with disabilities who lived there.

The idea of visiting the Centre pour Handicapés made me nervous. I thought of Mama Kavira's grandson with his neck that refused to hold up his head. A few months earlier I had taken the little boy to the hospital and paid for a variety of x-rays. The doctors had given him a neck brace, but the pain of wearing it made him cry. And after months of doctor's visits, my assistance had been utterly useless. I had seen the challenges of life in Goma and could only imagine how much greater they were for those with disabilities. I wasn't sure I had anything to offer.

Still, a sewing group interested me.

One day, I decided to pass by the Center on my way to Virunga Market. It was a reconnaissance mission of sorts. I would just peer in and see what I found inside.

I walked the three kilometers (two miles) to the Center, turning right off the main road, heading north toward the volcano, and crossing a wide swath of lava rock. The sun beat down, and I grew more and more nervous as I walked. Finally, I arrived at a big metal gate. I pushed the gate in, half holding my breath. As the gate opened, I found a series of low buildings painted in white with a neat blue trim. In the very corner of the property was a small, sturdy cement building. The door was flung open and I could see sewing machines inside. I could hear voices singing and laughing.

I walked into the building and found several young women sitting at sewing machines, their boisterous voices filling the air. "Karibu!" they called out to me, having no idea who I was. "Welcome!"

I asked to speak with the woman who organized the sewing project—the woman my husband had met. But she wasn't in the sewing shop that day. I decided to talk to the young women who were in front of me.

"Jina langu Dawn," I said to one of the women. "My name is Dawn."

"Jina langu Argentine," she replied in a bold voice.

"Argentina?" I asked in surprise, wondering how a South American country fit into this corner of the world.

She laughed, throwing her head back to reveal sparkling white teeth. Then she placed her hand on my arm and looked at me encouragingly.

"Ar-gen-tine," she said in a loud voice, enunciating each syllable. Her easy laughter and expressive face pulled me toward her.

"Unatoka wapi?" I asked in my basic Swahili. "Where are you from?"

She smiled and answered. "Nimetoka mbali."—"I have come from far."

Across from Argentine sat another young woman. She was following the conversation and nodding pleasantly, but her foot never stopped moving on the treadle beneath her sewing machine.

"Jina lako nani?" I asked as I approached her. "What is your name?"

She smiled shyly. "Jina langu Mapendo." "My name is Mapendo."

"Mapendo," I repeated, my face lighting up. It was a word I was familiar with. Mapendo means "love" in Swahili. "That is a good name!" I said. She smiled in response, as her hands fed cloth through her sewing machine.

I talked to Argentine and Mapendo for a while. I spoke enough Swahili to get through a general conversation, though always with lots of misunderstandings and laughter. Somewhere during that first year I'd learned to hear that laughter more as encouragement than mockery. The truth was that the people of Goma were almost always enthusiastic about my attempts at Swahili, "Unafanya vizuri *saaanaaaa*," they would say, drawing out the last word for emphasis. "You are doing *very* well"—more a reflection of their good-natured surprise at my attempt than an assessment of my actual language skills.

I also talked to two other women who were there, Berthe and Bernadette, and several men. They were all gracious and hospitable. After a while I thanked them and started to leave.

Just as I reached the door, Argentine's voice called me back. "Dada! Dada!" her voice rang out. "Sister! Sister!" She had already abandoned any attempt at my name, too short to roll off the tongue in Swahili.

"Tukule pa moja," she said. "Let's eat together."

Argentine had pushed her chair back from the sewing machine, and only then did I see that she was sitting on top of cushions. Up to this point I had entirely forgotten that I was at a center for people with disabilities. Now, my eyes took in Argentine's tiny frame and her legs that didn't reach the floor. She was still sitting on her chair, adjusting the metal leg braces hidden underneath her African skirt. She straightened her legs, and with a click she locked the metal leg braces in place. Grabbing her crutches, she stood up, and I realized that at her tallest, she didn't even reach my shoulders. But there was something about the way Argentine stood that made her appear larger than life. I knew instantly that no matter how tall the rest of the world was, Argentine believed herself to be the perfect size.

"Karibu," she said, gesturing to one of the tables. All the women gathered around. The men had disappeared to somewhere else. In the center of the table was a large plastic plate, piled high with beans and potatoes. Next to the plate of food was a pile of forks and two plastic mugs of water. Argentine said a prayer, her confident voice rising to the sky. And then we all began to eat, laughing and joking as we shared that single plate of food.

After a while I noticed Mapendo stealing glances in my direction. She appeared focused on my fork, undistracted by the laughter swirling around us. My eye caught hers.

"Dada, haukule," she said. "Sister, you are not eating." Her voice was quiet but firm. She was issuing a statement rather than a question.

I knew that I had eaten plenty. I motioned to my section of the plate, planning to demonstrate that it was nearly empty.

But my new friend was faster than me. Mapendo had already pushed more beans and potatoes onto my side of the plate, and I found myself gesturing directly at a new pile of food. I started to protest, then caught sight of the proud smile dancing on Mapendo's broad face. I picked up my fork and continued to eat, soaking in the warmth of my new friends.

CHAPTER TWENTY-ONE

Cutting Cloth Straight

On that first visit to the sewing cooperative, I learned that Argentine's disability was the result of polio. When she contracted polio as a young child, her leg muscles atrophied, leaving her with pencil-thin legs, too weak to bear her own weight. In order to stand, she wore heavy metal leg braces on both of her legs. The leg braces themselves seemed to weigh almost as much as Argentine's tiny frame. Watching Argentine move was like watching a miracle. She would stand rooted to the ground, with her braces locked into place and wooden crutches under both arms. Anyone watching her would think that she was stuck to the ground. And then, with no warning, she would explode into movement, bearing all her weight on her upper body, rising into the air and swinging both legs forward in one fluid motion. The heavy leg braces were rendered weightless under her command.

Mapendo, on the other hand, never soared. She never careened forward with both feet in the air. She moved like a different kind of miracle—the kind that it is easy to miss. At the age of eleven she had been hit by a motorcycle and her leg had broken in two places. She hadn't been able to get to a hospital and the leg healed badly. She wore a metal leg brace on her injured leg and used forearm crutches that seemed to leave her perpetually leaning forward. Mapendo had an athletic build and there was a solidness to her movements. While Argentine was like a bird caught in flight, Mapendo moved so smoothly and efficiently along the ground, that I often forgot about her disability altogether.

Both Mapendo and Argentine were in their early twenties, with Mapendo two years older than Argentine. They had lived at the Center for much of their teenage years. At the Center they had learned to read and write. They had undergone operations on their legs and hips and then learned to walk with braces and crutches. After more than five years at the Center, they had both finished their sewing training. Now these young women were trying to forge independent lives for themselves. The sewing cooperative where they were working was independent of the Center, just sharing space inside the property.

There were two other women in the group, Bernadette and Berthe. Bernadette sewed on a hand-crank sewing machine like Argentine's, with cushions piled on her chair and crutches leaning nearby. She also had a boisterous spirit, quick with witty commentary on whatever was going on. She was good friends with Berthe who sat quietly perched on the top of tables nearby, knitting baby clothing. Berthe didn't know how to sew, but she liked spending her day with the group. There were several men who seemed to manage the group and who also cut the cloth.

Occasionally the woman who had started the group would stop by. She had a full-time job at one of the aid organizations on the other side of town and was also involved with several other projects supporting the disabled community, so I didn't see her often in the sewing shop.

On my first visit I showed Argentine, Mapendo, and Bernadette an example of a small cloth purse and asked if they could sew something similar. The first purses came out with twisted straps and twirled around endlessly. But soon my new friends had mastered the purses, and I began placing bulk orders, planning to take the colorful little purses back with me to the United States to see if I could sell them. Each time my friends finished a set of purses, I would place cash in their hands. "You did the work. You get the money," I would say.

But soon I realized that they didn't really get to keep the money, no matter what I said, or what language I said it in.

"Ju ya nini?" I demanded. "Why not?"

"Look, Dada, we don't cut the cloth. One of the men cuts the cloth and then we sew it, so we have to pay them," Argentine explained in Swahili, her voice eager to please.

Seeing the puzzled look on my face, she flashed her brilliant white smile and reached out for my arm. "Hakuna shida," she said, laughing.

"Hakuna shida" means "No problem." It is one of the most common phrases in Goma. It seems to apply to almost all situations.

"Why do the men cut the cloth?" I demanded.

"Well...look..." Argentine said lightly. "Maybe we are not strong enough. Because of our disabilities we don't stand straight, so maybe we won't be able to cut the cloth straight." The explanation seemed completely out of sync with everything about Argentine's presence.

"But aren't the men in the group also disabled?" I asked in indignation.

"Yes. But they are men. They are strong," Argentine replied, puffing herself up in demonstration.

My eyes grabbed Argentine's eyes. "But *can* you cut the cloth straight?" I asked.

"Oh yes, of course we can," Argentine said with an easy laugh, as though my question fell from the sky, entirely unrelated to any other part of this conversation. To her, whether she could do the task was entirely beside the point. While I was concerned with independence, she was concerned with maintaining relationships. Underneath her buoyant enthusiasm, Argentine has always been navigating the currents of waters that I can't even see.

CHAPTER TWENTY-TWO

Other Dreams

There were so many things I didn't know about Argentine and Mapendo's lives—so many things I assumed. I learned that they had just started sewing in this cooperative a few months earlier. In fact, the whole cooperative had just recently started. Originally, when they started sewing with the cooperative, they had both been living with Mapendo's sister on the outskirts of Goma, but the cost of transportation to the sewing workshop each day had proven impossibly high. Argentine and Mapendo had asked for permission to clear out the back room of the workshop and put a single bed inside. There was no space for two beds.

That is when I met Argentine and Mapendo. They were living in that back room and sewing in the cooperative. I knew they had been treated at the Center and now here they were working and living at the Center. I connected dots that had never been connected, imagining they had transferred easily from treatment and sewing classes to independence. I imagined their lives laid out before them in some form of a logical plan.

But the truth, I would learn later, was that they had already been running all their lives, sometimes unsure where the next meal or the next place to stay might come from. Sharing a single bed in the back of this workshop did not constitute a home they could count on. They dreamed of a place of their own.

After a few months we looked for a place, settling on a half-built wooden structure, where the landlord promised to use our advance payment to pour concrete over the dirt floor. Argentine and Mapendo moved into the house along with Berthe and Bernadette. They kept ties with the original sewing cooperative, agreeing to help anytime there was extra work. But the women smiled proudly as they moved into their new home. They hung white lacey curtains from the doorway, and every time someone stopped by to visit, they called out, "Karibu kwetu." "Welcome to our home."

CHAPTER TWENTY-THREE

Quiet

Usually when I visited their new home, my friends would be sitting at their sewing machines or standing at the table cutting cloth. Mapendo's seven-year-old niece, Neema, had come to live with them, and often she would be sitting on a low stool next to a charcoal stove, frying onions or boiling beans. Usually there were other people visiting the house, friends and family members who laughed and joked as the work carried on. Much like the streets of Goma, their home felt like a party to me.

Sometimes, I caught my friends in a quieter moment. One time, Argentine was home alone, sitting on her bed in a small back room. Without her metal braces her legs looked tiny, and, in the moment, she was quiet and subdued, stripped of her public persona. "Dada, let me tell you about my life," she said, patting an empty space on her bed and flashing her smile. I sat on her bed, leaning my back against the raw wood boards behind me, and forgetting all the other things I had planned to do that day. "Dada, do you know where Masisi is?" Argentine began.

CHAPTER TWENTY-FOUR

Argentine

Argentine grew up in Masisi, a rural territory in Congo (then Zaire). At three or four years old, she contracted polio. Her family was living in a very rural area, and they were poor. Without access to medical care, her legs curled up under her, and she resorted to crawling on her hands, dragging her legs behind her. Because of her disability, Argentine was unable to start school or even leave the house. She grew up inside her small rural home, singing and praying, or sitting in the sun just outside. When other children her age started going to school, Argentine's heart broke. The whole neighborhood would empty out, and her mother would go out to farm, and she would be alone in the house.

The solitude pained Argentine's boisterous spirit. She would sit outside, eagerly waiting for the neighborhood children to return at noon. When they returned, she would call out to them, "How was school today?" Argentine learned to joke with the other children, throwing back her head in laughter, smiling radiantly, drawing them towards her.

Argentine's family was from an area rich with fertile farmland and beautiful pastures. However, by the time Argentine was born in the late 1980s, Congo (then Zaire) was in economic decline. President Mobutu Sese Seko had ruled the country by one-party dictatorship since 1965, when he seized power with a military coup d'état. Through his totalitarian and predatory regime (which enjoyed strong support from the US, France, and Belgium), Mobutu amassed a large personal fortune and created an environment of pervasive corruption, effectively coopting the function of state institutions for personal benefit. He employed a strategy of divide and rule, exacerbating ethnic tensions in a nation of more than 250 ethnic groups. This fomenting of ethnic tensions became particularly problematic in eastern Congo where the seeds of ethnic tension had been planted by colonial era land policy, and conflicts around ethnicity and citizenship had been brewing for decades. As the Mobutu regime began to collapse in the 1990s, eastern Congo spiraled toward chaos with the increased arming of rebel groups and local militias in the region.

Argentine's family found themselves unable to farm their rural land because of the increasing insecurity. They moved to the center of a small village, where they lived in a hut by the side of the road, next to a stream. But even in the village, conditions were getting worse. Young men wielding machetes or guns would arrive in the town, pillaging from house to house. The names of the groups changed over the years, as did the various alliances. But the effect on the local population was always the same. Families lived in terror, waiting for the next attack. The people of Masisi grew up fearing that their sons would be kidnapped and forced to fight. They feared that their daughters would be carried off by the boys with guns. They taught their children to flee for their lives. When rumors of armed men nearby started to circulate, the local population would abandon their houses and flee into the trees. Families would pre-arrange locations in the forest to meet. A large family would plan to separate, knowing that too many children in one hiding location was sure to attract attention.

By the time Argentine was eight or nine, it seemed like her family had to flee from their home almost every week. As soon as Argentine's mother heard rumors of danger, she would carry Argentine into the woods, feeling the weight of an eight-year-old child on her back. After hiding Argentine in the woods, she would then double back to help her younger children. Some of the neighbors had already begun to say, "Why do you keep carrying that disabled child like that? She can't fetch water for you. She'll never get married. What can she do for you? Leave her behind and worry about your other children." But Argentine's mother ignored their comments. She would take one of the younger children and Argentine together into the woods to keep each other company. Sometimes, when she could hear gunfire, she would dig a little hole and cover it with banana leaves.

"Lie here," she would tell them. "The bullets won't reach you in this hole." And then she would disappear into the distance, to find food or to check on her other children.

It wasn't always easy to stay ahead of the attacks. One night, Argentine's entire family was at home sleeping when they awoke to a large thud. Armed men had broken down the door and rushed into the room. "Everyone out of bed," they called, shining flashlights in their faces. One of the attackers grabbed Argentine's father and pushed him under a low coffee table. Argentine's father was trapped flat on his back, his nose an inch from the underside of the table, his arms pinned by his sides. He could feel the cold metal of a gun pressed to his temple. "Tell us where your money is," the attacker demanded.

Another shadowy figure grabbed one of Argentine's siblings, a boy of three or four years old. The man held a knife to the little boy's naked belly and looked directly at Argentine's mother. "Do what we say or your son dies."

Luckily, Argentine's father had money that day. He gave it to the armed men. If not, they might have killed him. As it was, the men took the money, backed out the door, and disappeared into the night.

CHAPTER TWENTY-FIVE

Who Do They Say That We Are?

1999

A few years later, Argentine was home alone with her younger brother. She was eleven years old. Her parents had taken the other children and gone to visit a family member in another village for a few days.

It was evening and Argentine and her brother were getting ready for the evening meal. Suddenly, a group of men in heavy coats and big boots pushed through the door. They lit up the room, spinning flashlights around, checking the corners, until their flashlights settled on the two children in one corner.

"Come here!" one of the man shouted at Argentine.

She crawled toward him.

He shined his flashlight straight into her face so that she was forced to look away into the night.

"Look at you," he murmured. "You are a good girl, aren't you?" he said, his eyes sliding down her body.

"But what's wrong with your legs?" he asked, suddenly surprised.

"I am disabled," Argentine whispered, her heart pounding.

"Never mind that," he continued. "Sit down here by the fire and help us peel these cooking bananas," the man said. Argentine sat by the fire, trembling. The man handed her a large stalk of bananas.

He watched her silently. "Don't be afraid of us, we won't kill you," he said. "Look at my face. Do you know me?" the man demanded. Argentine kept her eyes down and shook her head no.

"But you must hear what they say in this village," the man pressed on. "Who do they say that we are?"

Argentine swallowed, her throat gone dry. She tried to shake her head, but the man was animated now and wouldn't let up. "I promise we won't kill you, just tell me who they say that we are."

The truth is that it was not always clear who the attackers were. They came in darkness, shining flashlights in their victims' faces. There were a variety of rebel groups, mai-mai (local militia), and government soldiers who sometimes preyed on the village. But in this case Argentine heard the language the men were speaking. She knew who this group was. But she kept her face empty, and her voice soft and innocent, unwilling to utter the name of a group so deeply associated with massacres.

"I don't know who they say that you are," she replied.

"Well, what do they say that we do?"

Argentine's mind flashed with possible answers.

"Some say that you kill people," she began quietly, "but I don't know anything about that. I see that you pass through our village. I see you bring us bananas to eat," she finally answered, glancing at the bananas stewing with tomato and onion.

"What do you think?" the man said, jumping to his feet and showing his face in the light. "Am I a good person or a bad person?"

Argentine glanced again at the man, and suddenly noticed that he had had a black Bible in his hands. "Good person," she said in a voice that she hoped sounded confident.

"You see I have this Bible here. Maybe I am a pastor," he said, his face suddenly breaking into a grin. "Let me teach you about God," he began.

The man sat with Argentine for hours that night, questioning her about God, a catechism of sorts, as the bananas stewed, and the other men ate, their weapons resting to the side.

Some of the men lay down to sleep on Argentine's bed, others set up blankets on the floor. The night grew late.

"We have to believe in God," the man said, finally reaching the end of his catechism. "Take your brother and go into your parents' bedroom to sleep. We'll be gone in the morning," he told her.

Argentine moved toward the darkened bedroom, struggling to keep her breath steady.

But before she could reach the doorway, the man called out to her again, in a hushed voice. "But wait...you have to do one thing for me," he whispered, letting his eyes rest heavy on her face again.

Argentine shrank back. There was a long pause. There was nowhere to hide.

"Tell your mother to never leave you alone like this again. We didn't hurt you today. But not every man will be good like us," the man said.

With that, he turned back to the fire.

Argentine made her way to the bedroom and lay on the bed, unable to close her eyes in the dark. She prayed to God and listened to the quiet voices of men making their plans, her body stiff as a board, and her eyes on the shadow of the doorway.

Eventually she heard the front door shut. The men had left. She waited until morning, never sleeping at all.

In the first light of morning Argentine slid out of bed and fell to the floor, thanking God for his mercy. She made her way into the living room, which was empty now. On the table she found cans of tomato paste and a bag of salt, staples of any meal, an offering left by the men who had invaded.

Argentine opened the front door and pulled herself outside, craving the morning sunlight, warm and soft on her skin. As she pulled herself outside, she glanced over at her yard, noticing suddenly that her family's banana trees had been stripped bare. She understood then that the men had not brought bananas with them, as she had thought, but had ripped them from her own yard. Those bananas that might have fed her family for a week had disappeared in a single night, eaten by men hovering in the darkness, men whose faces she had never seen.

"Am I a good person or a bad person?" their leader had asked, shining the light in his own face.

"Good," she had answered, hoping it might somehow be the truth.

CHAPTER TWENTY-SIX

Faith

That year conditions became so bad in Argentine's village that many families resorted to living in the forests, abandoning their houses altogether.

Argentine's family had been living in the forest for several months, moving from one area to another. At one point they sought safety under a stand of tall trees, far out in the forest. The trees were so tall and so thick that if it rained, they wouldn't get wet underneath. They set up camp there, sleeping under those trees, and thinking it was a good spot. Then one day a relative came to visit them there. It was evening when they heard his footsteps, and his voice calling out.

"Miye huyu. Miye huyu. Usiogope."—"It's me. It's me. Don't be afraid," the relative whispered as he approached.

But when the relative arrived, he glanced quickly at the trees above and cried out.

"What have you done! You can't sleep here. These are the trees that are full of poisonous snakes!"

Argentine looked up at the trees, its branches reaching down to cover her. Just a moment, before she had felt comforted by the tree, but now it seemed dark and ominous.

"Tomorrow we will move," Argentine's mother said as the night closed in on them. "God will protect us tonight."

They slept that night, under those branches, watching shadows that danced like snakes. The next day Argentine's mother set out in search of a new hiding place. She left Argentine and one of her siblings behind under those tall trees, unable to carry Argentine to a place she hadn't yet found. "I'll come back as soon as I find a new hiding place," she promised Argentine.

Stuck under a tree of poisonous snakes, Argentine decided to fast and pray. Sometime amid her prayers she fell asleep. She dreamt of people in white clothes circling around her, looking at her legs. She startled awake from her dream, convinced that it was a sign.

When her mother returned, Argentine declared, "I have had a dream. We must go to Goma. There are people dressed in white who will help me there." She spoke with the confidence of a prophet.

Argentine had heard about Goma years before from a pastor who visited their local church. The pastor had asked Argentine's parents why they didn't take her to the Centre pour Handicapés in Goma.

"But we have no money, and the treatment there will be expensive," Argentine's mother had answered. But the words stayed in Argentine's heart, planted like a seed.

"Wait until we save up money, and then we will go," her mother responded.

They were living in the woods under trees filled with snakes. Argentine could see her fate written out. She knew there was no money and probably never would be.

"Niko na imani." "I have faith," she replied. "We must go now."

Argentine and her mother had been having this conversation back and forth for months. It would be an enormous undertaking. Argentine's mother could barely carry Argentine on her back for a short distance. How could they get to Goma, well over 150 kilometers (93 miles) away? They were far out in the forest, and Argentine's mother had other children to worry about and a baby tied to her back.

But something in Argentine's voice convinced her mother that day.

"I have faith. I have seen it," Argentine told her mother as they sat under the tree with the snakes hanging over them.

"Did you really see it?" her mother asked.

"I have seen it," Argentine responded. Together they began to plan.

CHATPER TWENTY-SEVEN

The Road to Goma

December 2001

Argentine's mother kissed her other children goodbye. She left them there, in the woods, in the care of their father and begged them to stay safe. She carried her youngest child, still a baby, on her back. Some men from church accompanied them on the first part of their journey, carrying Argentine through the forest, until they reached a dirt path. There they had arranged for a *chukudu*, a large wooden scooter that men usually pushed along the roadside, loaded with bananas or charcoal. They balanced Argentine on the scooter and pushed her forward. Progress was slow. In some areas the path was too steep, and in other areas the path disappeared under water. The men would pick Argentine up, carry her forward, and then place her back on the wooden scooter. Finally, they stopped.

"This is as far as we can push you," they said. "We must return to our own families now."

Argentine and her mother thanked the men, then huddled by the dirt roadside, trying to decide what to do next. There was no way that Argentine's mother could carry her further. In the distance, they saw a bicycle propped outside a house. Argentine's mother knocked on the door.

"Please help me take my daughter to the nearest town," she begged the people inside that house.

The strangers agreed to carry Argentine and her mother on the back of bicycles to the town of Mweso. Argentine and her mother stayed in Mweso a week while they tried to find transportation to Goma. Finally, they found a truck traveling to Goma. The truck was piled high with goods. Argentine and her mother joined the other passengers perched gingerly on top of the overloaded truck, hugging themselves in the cold open air and praying they would make it safely to Goma.

The path to Goma was roughly one hundred kilometers (sixty-two miles) on a road that barely existed. Sometimes the road became so full of mud that the tires spun hopelessly. Sometimes the truck broke down. When the truck ground to a halt, the passengers climbed down from their high perches and created impromptu camps along the side of the road, pulling their small charcoal stoves down from the truck, sending for supplies from nearby villages, and gathering together for warmth in the nighttime air. Eventually, the truck would start again, and their journey would continue. Finally, after three or four days, they arrived in Goma.

"Twahageze."—"We have arrived," Argentine's mother whispered, glancing about her at the swirling city. It was the end of the day, and the market district was full of people shouting. The green hills of Masisi were far away.

Standing there, Argentine's mother weighed her options. She had no idea how to get to the Centre pour Handicapés and no money. It was getting dark.

Soon, a disabled woman wheeled up to Argentine and her mother. She was driving a *kinga*, an oversized tricycle. Kingas are a common solution for people with disabilities in Congo. They have hand pedals and a platform in the back for carrying goods. Many people with disabilities in Goma use their kingas as a source of work, peddling goods back and forth over the border between Rwanda and Congo.

This woman was carrying soda bottles in the back of her kinga. She greeted Argentine and her mother warmly.

"Tomorrow I will help you get to the Center. But right now, you must find a place to sleep for the night," the woman said, glancing at the darkening sky. "Mama, take your baby," she said, motioning to the baby on Argentine's mother's back. "Go and find somewhere to sleep for yourselves. I will take Argentine on my kinga to my house. She will sleep at my house tonight, and we will meet you here on this exact street corner again in the morning."

Argentine pulled herself onto the woman's kinga and nestled her small frame between crates of soda bottles. At eleven or twelve years old, she was sitting in the middle of an unfamiliar city, trusting herself into the hands of a stranger. She didn't even have the confidence of a common language. Her family spoke a language at home that was common in the high hills of Masisi, but in Goma she needed Swahili. She tried to remember the bits and pieces of Swahili she had learned. Then she waved goodbye to her mother. "We'll see each other again in the morning!" Argentine called out. Then she leaned back onto the soda bottles, confident she would see her mother again. This stranger driving the kinga was disabled. *People with disabilities are my family*, Argentine thought to herself.

At the house, the woman proved to be kind and generous, and Argentine slept well. The next morning, they climbed on the kinga and headed back to the street corner to find Argentine's mother. Suddenly there was a thud. The kinga's wheel had burst, grounding them on the side of the road. The woman looked back and forth, from the flat tire to Argentine. Finally, she told Argentine to sit by the side of the road and wait. "I'll be back," she promised. "I am going to find help to fix my kinga," she said, as she called for boys to push the kinga to a shop for repair.

Argentine sat by the side of the road, watching crowds pass her by, waiting for the woman to return. Soon the sun was high in the sky. Argentine began picturing her mother's face, fallen and tear stained, waiting for a daughter who never appeared. The afternoon sun settled into the sky and the woman still had not returned. The roads began to fill with the bustle of late afternoon. A disabled man in a kinga finally happened upon her, wheeling by in his own kinga.

"Mtoto, unafanya nini?" the man asked Argentine. "Child, what are you doing?"

"Nimepoteza mama wangu." Argentine whispered back to him in shaky Swahili. "I lost my mother."

"But where are you from?"

"I am from Masisi," she answered. "We ran from the war."

"Masisi," the man said with a sigh. "Where were you trying to go?"

"We were going to the Centre pour Handicapés."

"But I can't take you to the Centre pour Handicapés now," the man said, shaking his head. "If you arrive at the Center without your mother, they will send you away, and you will be lost all over again. I will take you to Caritas Hospital. There is a mzungu there who helps people, especially abandoned children."

Argentine's breath caught in her throat. She had never met a mzungu, but all her life she had heard stories. "Wazungu wanakula watoto," they had said in her village. "White people eat children," parents told their misbehaving children. Argentine looked from the stranger to the darkening street. She took a deep breath and got on the back of his kinga. *Disabled people are like family, even if I don't know them yet,* she told herself again.

The man peddled slowly over the bumpy lava rock roads. He turned down one street after another, and soon Argentine had no idea where she was. Finally, they arrived at a gate. "Go up to that gate. Tell them your name. Tell them you are from Masisi. Everyone knows how you have suffered in Masisi. They will open the gate and let you in." Then he lowered his voice. "But you mustn't tell them I brought you here." The man left Argentine at the gate and wheeled quickly away.

Argentine pulled herself toward the gate on her hands, her bent legs dragging behind her.

As she approached the red gate, a guard swung open the door and listened to Argentine's tearful story in broken Swahili. After hearing Argentine's story, the guard sent for Sister Louise, the white nun who worked at the hospital.

Soon Sister Louise arrived. She stepped close to Argentine. "What is your name, my child? Where are you from?" Sister Louise began in Swahili. Argentine heard the kindness layered in her voice. She heard the Swahili rolling off her tongue, and she found her breath again, letting go of the fears of her childhood.

"Are you sure your mother is coming back for you?" Sister Louise asked gently.

Argentine straightened up. "My mother is coming back for me. She loves me," Argentine insisted.

"Don't worry, tomorrow I will help you find your mother," Sister Louise promised.

That night Sister Louise brought Argentine fish to eat. In the morning she sent another woman with porridge and bread. "If your mother doesn't come soon, I will take you to the radio station, and they will put you on the radio to make an announcement," Sister Louise told Argentine. Argentine's body froze again at the thought. She wondered what it meant to put someone on the radio.

Just as Argentine sat there, wondering about the radio, she heard the front gate opening and people arriving. Argentine looked out the doorway to see the shape of a kinga pulling through the gate. Her eyes raced up the metal body of the kinga, and there was the woman from the previous day, her wheel newly fixed. Argentine looked to the side, and saw her own mother standing there, exhaustion and fear written on her face. Argentine and her mother caught sight of each other. Shouting with joy, they collapsed into each other's arms.

Sister Louise heard the noise and peeked outside. "Argentine, is this your mother?" she asked, glancing at Argentine's mother, her face stained with tears.

"I can see now that you were right. Your mother loves you very much," Sister Louise said.

CHAPTER TWENTY-EIGHT

Centre pour Handicapés

Sister Louise sat with Argentine and her mother that day. "But how did you escape the war? How did you get to Goma?" The questions poured from Sister Louise.

After hearing Argentine and her mother's lives laid out before her, Sister Louise stood up. "I will take you to the Center myself. And if they agree to treat you, I will pay for the treatment." Argentine's heart soared. *God brought us here*, Argentine thought to herself.

For two weeks, Argentine waited for a consultation at the Center. Finally, the day for the consultation arrived. Argentine lay on a bed and the medical staff circled around her, dressed in white, Argentine's dream suddenly come to life. "I told you I saw it," Argentine said to her mother.

The staff at the Center agreed to take Argentine in for treatment on two conditions. The first condition was that Argentine's mother stay in Goma to care for her. "You can't abandon your child here. You must stay," a serious-looking man said, looking at her mother over his glasses. Then he turned to Argentine. "And you? Will you be patient?" he asked Argentine, trying to establish whether she would be strong enough to undergo the painful treatment process.

"Yes, I will be patient," Argentine assured him, unable yet to imagine what lay in store for her.

The staff at the Center gave Argentine a bed. Their first goal was to straighten her legs, which had contracted into a bent position due to muscle atrophy. Men in white coats pulled at her legs straightening them just a centimeter. Then they slathered her tiny, bent legs in plaster and put a rod in the space between the back of her thigh and the back of her calf, prying the gap open just a bit. The next Friday they returned. They cut the plaster, pried her leg a little straighter, and then replacing the plaster and wooden rod. Every Friday they returned, until Argentine grew to hate Fridays. "Don't give up now," the other girls would tell Argentine. "My legs were once bent like yours. Look how I am standing now," they would say.

Argentine lived in a room full of teenage girls. Some had already undergone treatment; others were in various stages of treatment. Finally, after more than a year of successive casts, Argentine's tiny legs had returned to a straightened position. The staff at the center took her to a hospital to have an operation on her hips.

"When you wake from the operation, don't even think of sitting up. You will be in a cast from foot to chest," the doctors warned her.

After the operation, Argentine opened her eyes and stared straight at the ceiling. For three months she would lie in that bed and stare at the ceiling, unable to move her body from chest down. She started to sing the songs she had learned in church. She sang Psalm 23 over and over again.

Bwana ndiye mchungaji wangu,
Sitakosewa na kitu...

The Lord is my shepherd,
I shall not want...

After the plaster was removed, her legs were fitted with metal braces. At first, she felt great, seeing her legs stretched out before her. But then doubt filled her heart. "What if I am not strong enough to walk?" she whispered to her friends in the quiet of the night.

First, Argentine practiced strapping her metal braces on her legs and leaning on a walker, pulling herself upright. She went up and down. Up and down. But then when she tried to do the same thing with her crutches, her back wobbled from side to side like it was blowing in the wind, and she collapsed downward.

Her thoughts returned. *What if I am not strong enough*? For months she practiced standing and taking one small step and then another. Sometimes her crutches slipped out from underneath her and she spilled to the floor. The other girls nearby would collapse into laughter, and so would Argentine. They all fell sometimes, and they all laughed. The laughter helped them to get back up.

After months of practice, Argentine learned to walk, seeing the world from higher than ever before.

And then, for a moment, everything seemed possible. She learned to root herself to the ground, and then fling her legs into the air, as I would see her do on her crutches years later. She began the sewing program at the Center, designed to give her a concrete skill with which she could reenter the world. Then, just as she was beginning the sewing program, a staff member at the Center came to see her one day.

"Where is your mother?" the woman asked angrily. "She left without our permission. And she hasn't returned to visit you.

She has abandoned you here and we have no funding to continue your sewing program."

Tears of shame and horror burned down Argentine's cheeks.

"My mother has not abandoned me," she insisted. "She loves me. She would never abandon me," Argentine explained, knowing that her mother had returned to Masisi to care for her many other children. But there was no use explaining. Not knowing where to go, Argentine packed her bags and hugged her friends goodbye. She could not go back to the small village where her family lived. It was high in the hills, and she could never walk up those hills with her metal leg braces and crutches. Eventually a woman from church offered to let Argentine stay with her. The woman's husband was a pastor, and their family was poor, with many people in every bed and many mouths to feed. Still, when Argentine arrived at the door, this woman chose to open it.

"You are welcome here," the woman said.

"I won't take up hardly any space," Argentine whispered back.

A year of Argentine's life disappeared that way, in the darkness of having nowhere to go. And then one day, the Center called Argentine back, saying they had found funding to pay for her to return.

Argentine returned to the Center and began to learn to sew.

For three years she learned to sew, memorizing sewing patterns in her head, tracing lines with chalk, and then cutting the cloth, stitching pieces together while she laughed with friends. She was her buoyant self. But every night lying in bed she returned to the same question. *Where can I find a home?* She knew she wouldn't be allowed to stay in the Center much longer, and she was determined not to get stuck again.

She came up with a plan to ask her parents to move to a larger village called Kitchanga on the main road. She begged them to move, and eventually they agreed, with the help of a little money that Argentine received as a gift from friends.

After that, Argentine felt better. She knew she had somewhere to return to. After three years in the sewing program, it was finally time for Argentine to receive her certificate and move out. The staff at the Center gave Argentine a sewing machine and some cloth. She called someone who lived in Kitchanga to deliver a message to her family down the road.

"Tell them I am ready to come home," Argentine said.

CHAPTER TWENTY-NINE

A Wife

January 2007

When Argentine arrived in Kitchanga, she could feel the tension rippling through the air. Kitchanga, and surrounding Rutshuru territory, was a stronghold area for Laurent Nkunda. Nkunda had led rebel troops in the Second Congo War. In 2003, when the war officially ended, Nkunda and his troops had joined the newly integrated Congolese army. However integration of Nkunda's units had broken down, and he and many of his men had withdrawn to his highland strongholds around Kitchanga where they were in the process of forming a new rebel group.

Argentine set up a small sewing shop on the main road and attempted to go on with life. She sang in the church choir. At the rehearsals she became friends with a young girl named Chantal.

One day, Argentine was sitting outside her sewing shop when Chantal passed by on the street, shadowed closely by a high-ranking soldier.

"How are you?" Argentine called out to her friend.

"I am good," Chantal replied. And then she paused, throwing a look quickly behind her. "I will come and visit you tomorrow. I want to have you sew something for me. I will come with my husband tomorrow."

"What?! You have a husband now?" Argentine asked the young girl in alarm. Chantal was thirteen years old. The girl nodded her head and disappeared down the road alongside the soldier.

The next day Chantal arrived with her husband, the same high-ranking soldier she had been walking with the day before. Her "husband" stood watchfully in the doorway. In fact, Argentine would never see her young friend again without soldiers of some sort accompanying her.

A few months later, Chantal and her husband arrived in Argentine's sewing shop with a proposal.

"I want to have you sew shirts for the wives of my soldiers," Chantal's husband said to Argentine.

Argentine looked up at this man, with his guns and his uniform. She kept her face pleasant and searched her mind for an appropriate response. She found only one.

"Yes. Of course," she said, knowing she might never be paid for her work.

One by one the wives of the soldiers began to arrive in her sewing shop. Many were young girls. Argentine welcomed them, wrapping her measuring tape around their chests and their waists.

"This shirt will look very good on you," she promised them all.

Sometimes, soldiers with no wives also came by the shop. Sometimes the men just wanted Argentine to sew their shoes back together. Argentine sat staring at the soldiers' broken-down shoes. *The life of a soldier is very difficult*, Argentine thought to herself, looking at these men who were often no more than boys.

Sometimes the men seemed to be looking for something beyond stitching. There was one soldier who started to come by the workshop again and again. He would sit there for hours while Argentine sewed.

"Hey you!" he would call to one of the kids playing outside. When a boy came near, the soldier would hand him some money. "Go and get me a beer." The little boy would return with the beer and the soldier would sit next to Argentine and drink his beer.

Argentine grew nervous. She stopped going to her workshop on the main road. She stayed home at her mother's house, far off the main road. One evening she heard knocking at the door of the house. She opened the door, leaning on her crutches, a smile frozen on her face. The soldier from her sewing shop had found her home. Now he was standing in the doorway.

"What are you doing here?" Argentine asked, with a voice that might have trembled.

"I've come to visit you," he said, stepping inside and sitting down.

After that, the soldier started stopping by her house regularly.

Argentine lay awake at night, just like she had under the tree filled with snakes. She calculated her limited resources and played out possible scenarios, trying to imagine a way forward.

Finally, she came up with a plan. "Mama," she said to her mother. "From now on, every time the soldier comes to our house, I will get in bed and pretend to be sick. You just tell him I am sick. But whatever you do, don't let him take me to a hospital," she told her mother.

The next time the soldier came to the house, he stared at Argentine lying in her bed. Then he looked at Argentine's mother. "What do you mean your daughter is sick?" he asked skeptically. "What's wrong?

"Oh, we aren't really sure," Argentine's mother answered, her voice trailing off.

The soldier returned again and again, bearing medicines of various sorts. Argentine remained in the house, giving up her sewing altogether.

One day, on her way to the market, Argentine's mother passed by the soldier in the street.

"Why do you keep visiting my daughter like this?" she asked the man.

"She's my wife," the soldier answered. "One day I will come in a truck. I will carry her and her kinga away."

Argentine's mother ran back to the house that day, her hands trembling. "We must send you back to Goma! You can't stay here," she said to Argentine. The roads between Kitchanga and Goma were unsafe to travel, with rebels holding some areas and the government forces holding others, and few buses traveling in between.

"Maybe your brothers can push you in your kinga back to Goma," Argentine's mother suggested.

Argentine shook her head. "We'll only lose my brothers that way. They'll be forced into the forest to fight."

Finally, Argentine decided to seek help in the only way she knew how. She went to her friend Chantal and the soldier, for whom she had sewn so many shirts.

"Please help me get to Goma. I have to go!" Argentine threw herself on his mercy.

He looked over at her. "Do you see any bombs falling here? Aren't we keeping you safe here? Why do you want to run away? You will give our troops a bad name."

"No! No!" Argentine exclaimed. "I am not running away. I will be back within two weeks. Only, I need to return to the Centre pour Handicapés. I have a problem with my back."

The man considered Argentine's words, then relented.

"I will take you myself."

A few days later, Argentine climbed into a truck with that high-ranking soldier, wrapping a scarf around her head.

"This is my daughter," he said at each checkpoint, and they were waved through. Finally, they reached the edge of Sake. "I can take you no farther, he said, calling for a boy on a bicycle to carry her the rest of the way into Sake. She took a bus from Sake to Goma. That is how Argentine returned to Goma. She didn't return to Kitchanga.

A few months later, I met Argentine at the Center. "Umetoka wapi?" I asked in my simple Swahili. "Where have you come from?"

"Nimetoka mbali," Argentine replied, flashing her brilliant white smile. "I have come from far." It would be many years before I could begin to imagine how very far Argentine had already come.

CHAPTER THIRTY

Mapendo

If it took me a long time to comprehend Argentine's childhood, it took me even longer to imagine Mapendo's childhood. Argentine's childhood splintered early, with polio limiting her opportunities almost as long as she could remember. Mapendo watched her future slowly dissolve between her fingertips.

Mapendo's family is from Kimoka, a small village that sits high in the hills, five kilometers (three miles) above the larger town of Sake. Sake is twenty-three kilometers (fourteen miles) from the city of Goma, and it felt like Goma, caught amid conflict, poverty and hustle. But the village of Kimoka, up in the hills, felt like a different world entirely, with small thatched huts. Mapendo lived with her mother, father and older siblings in a small home, with aunts, uncles and cousins nearby. Her mother had born thirteen children. Three died in childhood, but ten remained. Their family owned a small plot of land to farm, way out in the distance. They often hiked out into the hills to farm during the day and returned to their hut at night. Their farm provided just enough food for their family to eat.

Mapendo was a healthy little girl, her parents' youngest child. When she was six years old, her mother registered her for school, just like her older siblings. Mapendo was excited to start first grade.

But one day, shortly after the start of the school year, the people of Kimoka awoke to find leaflets scattered on the dirt outside their homes.

Leave now. If you do not leave, we are coming to kill you, the leaflet read, and then it specified a date for the attack.

This was neither the first nor the last time they'd receive such leaflets. It was 1992 and tensions in the region had sparked. In the villages people from various ethnic groups lived side by side, sharing their lives. But in the surrounding area, rebel groups and militia groups formed along ethnic lines. The groups often threatened and attacked villages, in reprisal attacks that seemed to never end.

That day, after finding the leaflets threatening an attack, Mapendo's mother gathered the children and prepared to flee, bringing whatever food they had. Mapendo's father looked at her mother and shook his head. "How can I leave the only home we have?" He chose to stay behind, protecting what little they had.

Mapendo and her siblings fled with their mother down the hill toward the town of Sake. When they arrived in Sake, they knocked on the door of a woman from the market. That woman took them in, offering to let the family stay in her small living room. The children laid out little mats on the dirt floor.

In Kimoka, Mapendo's father stayed and guarded their home. His brothers had stayed too, in their own homes nearby. At night the men hid in the forest and waited there, watching for attackers. In the daytime they returned, staking claim to their homes.

The appointed date came and went. No attackers arrived. Another week followed. Silence still.

The men began returning to sleep in their homes at night, hoping the leaflets had been merely a scare tactic. And then one night, attackers swept through the village. They killed Mapendo's father and all but one of her uncles, slaughtering them with machetes in the night.

Down the hill in Sake, Mapendo's mother heard the news. She was a widow with many children to care for and a home where her husband's blood had sunk into the earth. She must have looked at her children, sleeping on the floor of someone else's house, and wondered where they could possibly go. But there was nowhere to go.

Mapendo never returned to school to start first grade. None of her siblings returned to school that year. Their fate had suddenly taken a sharp turn. For the next five years, Mapendo, her mother, and her siblings lived only to survive.

For months they would stay in the town of Sake, the entire family sleeping on someone else's dirt floor, laying out mats in the night, and then folding them up hurriedly the next morning, trying to disappear into the background of another family's life. The small home where they stayed was already stretched to the limits, and there wasn't even enough food to share. Still, the family had offered their roof. During the day, Mapendo's mother would take some of the children and hike for two or three hours, up the hills, past their village, to the plot of farmland. Each child carried a sweet potato and water. When they reached their small plot of land, they were exhausted and hungry. They would start a fire and roast their sweet potatoes, and then they would farm whatever they could, hoping to eke out just enough to survive.

Sometimes, when the fighting seemed to have calmed, the family would return to stay in their home in Kimoka again, trying to reestablish their life there. One night, Mapendo's mother had gone to the village on her own, leaving the children in Sake. She was standing in their small thatched home as evening approached. Somewhere deep inside, she knew that she couldn't stay in the house that night. She ran into the woods and hid herself under some branches. That night she saw the flashlights of attackers coming through the woods. She heard branches crunching underneath boots. She crouched on the ground and held her breath. The footsteps were nearly on top of her—the men's boots only inches from her body. And then, after what seemed like a lifetime, the men passed by, disappearing into the darkness.

Mapendo's childhood continued this way, living caught between Sake and Kimoka, between poverty and fear. The family was always too poor to rent a home in Sake and the village was always too unsafe to stay for long.

Even in the midst of war, Mapendo was an active child, strong and playful. One time, when she was eleven, she was playing ball in Sake with some other children. The game was animated, and Mapendo has always loved a good ball game. To this day, she lights up just describing the game. One of the players from the other team threw the ball far up into the air, and Mapendo raced after it. The ball, made of plastic bags and twine, spun out of reach, and Mapendo dashed across the road to retrieve it. Just then, a motorcycle taxi sped down the road. In an instant, the motorcycle hit Mapendo. She crumpled onto the ground. The motard sped away.

Mapendo's little friends crowded around her. They yelled for help, but Mapendo's mother was far away, farming their plot of land. A neighbor came out of his house. The man lifted Mapendo up, her leg broken in two places, and carried her into the house where they were staying. He laid her out on the dirt floor. Someone sent for another neighbor, not a medical doctor, but a local man who was known for straightening the bones of elderly people. He brought pieces of wood and pulled on Mapendo's leg, trying to realign her bones as she laid there. Then he fashioned a splint, placing a stick of wood on each side of the leg and tying it up with a brightly colored African cloth.

When Mapendo's mother returned to Sake that night, she looked at her daughter laid out on the floor. "We must return to Kimoka," she told Mapendo. Mapendo's mother didn't have money for a doctor or a hospital, but she knew that Mapendo couldn't stay immobile on someone else's floor. They had no other choice but to return to their home.

In the village, Mapendo laid on a mat on the floor, staring up at the thatch above her head. Her mother would leave food for her in the morning and then disappear to farm with Mapendo's older siblings. At night the family would return.

Sometimes, in the evening, the family would race back inside, clutching a leaflet like the one that had come years before, with warnings of an attack coming. Mapendo's mother would send her older children far into the forest. "Go as far as you can," she would say, especially to Mapendo's older brothers. Often, when attackers would hit a village, they would kill the men and teenage boys.

After she sent her older children far into the woods, she and Mapendo would hide for the night in some shrubs near the house. She couldn't carry Mapendo any farther, but she refused to leave her alone. In the darkness of night, those shrubs offered some measure of protection.

Then one day, disaster came in the daylight. It was sometime during the First Congo War, which ultimately toppled President Mobutu. Mapendo does not know exactly who the armed men were that stormed through her village as the sun shone brightly.

What she remembers is that she heard gunfire first. People were pouring into the forest, fleeing. And Mapendo could not flee.

Mapendo's mother sent her older children off, urging them to go as far and as fast as they could, handing them a kitenge (an African cloth) to cover themselves with at night.

Then she looked at Mapendo with her broken leg. They couldn't hide in the shrubs near the house in the daylight.

Mapendo's mother bent over and tried to lift Mapendo onto her back, but she couldn't. Instead Mapendo grabbed onto her mother's shoulder, sticking her broken leg off to one side. They struggled slowly down the road, with Mapendo leaning on her mother and limping forward. With every footstep they fell further behind their neighbors, and the sound of gunfire rang louder in their ears. Soon men were running past them. Other men came rushing behind them. Mapendo saw people fall in the streets—people hit by bullets.

Then, a soldier with a gun rushed up behind Mapendo's mother. He grabbed her arm and spun her around.

"Mama, where are you going?" the man demanded.

Mapendo's mother looked at him wordlessly.

"You can't walk like this. You will never make it." The man said, gesturing to Mapendo clutching at her mother's neck.

Mapendo's mother kept staring silently.

"Mama, you have to go back where you came from. We won't hurt you there," he promised.

Mapendo's mother, completely exhausted, turned around and began to walk with Mapendo back the way she had come. Armed men ran past her. Soon she saw a house with a door left open. Inside she saw people huddled in a corner. She walked into the house and joined the group, too exhausted and too scared to walk any farther.

The strangers made room for the new arrivals. “Sogea kidogo.” “Move over a little,” someone said. Then they sat there in silence, waiting for the storm to end.

CHAPTER THIRTY-ONE

Accepting the Crutches

Months after the accident, Mapendo still couldn't stand. Her leg had begun to heal, but the bones had never been set properly. She was left with a leg that could bear no weight, with the bones rubbing up against each other painfully.

Shortly after the accident, a neighbor had fashioned crutches out of wood and brought them to Mapendo. Mapendo stared at the wooden crutches and felt her stomach churn. The only people she had ever seen with crutches were old men. "No. I will get better," she said, pushing the crutches away.

Mapendo stayed at home for five years and never touched those crutches. She dreamed of one day being able to walk on her own again. She learned to knit and began knitting dish cloths and furniture coverings for her mother to sell at the market. Her childhood passed her by. *I'll never play again,* Mapendo thought to herself.

As the years went by, fighting near Kimoka began to calm, and some small measure of stability returned to the region. Finally, in December of 2002, an announcement was made at one of the churches that a group which helped disabled people would be coming to the area. Mapendo and her mother went for a consultation. A man named Papa Ruzi looked at Mapendo kindly. He told Mapendo that she might be able to get treatment at the Centre pour Handicapés in Goma. But first she had to get to Goma. Papa Ruzi looked at Mapendo's mother, studying her carefully, trying to gauge her commitment to her daughter.

"Mama, you have to find money to buy two bus tickets to Goma," he said to Mapendo's mother. She stared at her hands.

"You have to do it right away," he said, trying to push her to action. It was a Monday, and he told her she needed to get Mapendo to Goma by Thursday.

Mapendo's heart soared. *I will go to the Center. I will get better. I will play again,* she promised herself. With the optimism of a child, she imagined her leg magically recovering.

Mapendo's mother hiked into the hills that week. She had nothing on the farm to sell—nothing that would provide enough for their tickets to Goma. But on one side of their plot of land was a line of trees. She had planted those trees with her husband when they were still young, planning to grow them tall and sell them for wood one day. The trees were still too small to chop down for wood, so Mapendo's mother sold the future rights to those trees and bought two tickets to Goma.

When they arrived at the Center, Mapendo and her mother knocked at the gate.

"Who has sent you?" the guard asked them skeptically.

"Papa Ruzi has sent us," Mapendo's mother answered. The gate swung open. They were given a room at the guest house behind the Center. Eventually, the doctors sent Mapendo for x-rays, then called Mapendo's mother in for interviews.

"Why didn't you bring in this child earlier?" the staff at the Center asked, weighing a mother's commitment to her daughter. They couldn't know how faithfully this mother had carried her daughter. Perhaps only Mapendo would ever know that.

"I had no money," Mapendo's mother replied.

"If we agree to treat your daughter here, you must agree to come back every month to visit her. Can you do this?" the staff asked.

"Yes, I will come," Mapendo's mother whispered softly, blinking tears from her eyes.

"We will take her," the staff said. Mapendo's mother sighed in relief, but when she returned to Mapendo that night, Mapendo grabbed onto her mother.

"Don't leave me here," Mapendo begged her mother. "I don't know these people. Don't leave me alone. Take me with you."

In all her life Mapendo had never been far from her mother.

Mapendo's mother left shortly after. "You will be okay," she promised. Every month Mapendo's mother made good on her promise. She came back to visit Mapendo in Goma, carrying a homemade drink called *mutobe*. Mutobe is made from bananas, mashed and fermented. Every month Mapendo's mother hiked into the hills to find a stalk of bananas. She carried them home, mashed them and sold mutobe in the market in Sake that week. When the mutobe was nearly all gone, she knew she had enough money to buy a ticket to Goma. She would buy a bus ticket and carry the last sip of mutobe for Mapendo to drink.

The staff at the Center began consulting the x-rays and considering what could be done for Mapendo's leg, and whether they could raise support for her. First, they sent Mapendo to literacy and sewing classes.

As classes started, the Center filled up with other young women on crutches, returning from a holiday break. Mapendo stared at the young women. For the first time in a long time, Mapendo began to imagine a future for herself. *There are girls just like me*, she thought.

Mapendo watched the other young women walking effortlessly on their crutches, pivoting in circles. Some of the girls visited Mapendo and told her how once, not too long ago, they too had been unable to walk.

Papa Ruzi, the man who had first met Mapendo in the village, visited Mapendo every day. After a while he brought crutches to Mapendo and handed them to her. Mapendo looked down, preparing to shake her head.

"What? A strong girl like you? You want to stay this way forever?" Papa Ruzi joked with Mapendo, playing off her competitive streak.

Reaching out, Mapendo took the crutches from him for the first time.

"Tuende," he said. "Let's go."

They walked around the Center, in and out of the buildings and across the green grass. Soon Mapendo found herself visiting the building that housed patients with the most severe disabilities. She learned to consider all that she had. She learned her smile could give the next person courage.

Somewhere in between the visits from girls on crutches, laughing and joking and moving so easily, and the visits to others who were more disabled than herself, Mapendo found community and with that she found the strength to carry on.

CHAPTER THIRTY-TWO

Sports

August 2008

In quiet moments, I sat with Argentine and Mapendo in that wooden house and listened to these stories of their childhood. With each story, I realized a little more how shocking it was that they had ever made it to Goma and that they had become independent young women, living on their own in this wooden house. When I first met them, I had taken their dreams of independence for granted, not realizing how hard fought those dreams were.

As the weeks passed by, I also noticed that on Friday afternoons they were often hurrying to finish their work and talking in hushed tones, laced with excitement. They were preparing to go somewhere.

"Where are you going?" I asked Mapendo.

"Kufanya sport," Mapendo replied. "To do sports."

I could hear the pride in her voice. But my mind couldn't fit the pieces together. I wondered if I had stumbled on a false cognate. What kind of sport could Argentine and Mapendo possibly have found to play in Goma?

The only sport I had seen played successfully in Goma was soccer, and it was played by young men racing chaotically across dirt fields. I glanced at Mapendo and Argentine in their metal leg braces. My curiosity piqued, I followed them out of the house.

"I am coming with you!" I said.

We called down the road to some motorcycle taxis, and the drivers came in a rush. Argentine took the first motorcycle taxi. "Jambo," she greeted her driver enthusiastically. Then, leaning her two wooden crutches against the motorcycle, she hoisted herself onto the back of the seat with a flourish, her tiny legs dangling off to the side. She gave her motard a friendly pat on the back, and triumphantly declared, "Tuende!"—"Let's go!"

Mapendo climbed on the next motorcycle, quietly greeting the driver and then leaning on her good leg as she nonchalantly slid onto the seat. As the motorcycle pulled away, I watched her riding sidesaddle. I could only imagine how easy it would be to fall over backward. As my friends disappeared down the road, I climbed onto the remaining motorcycle and crossed one leg over the seat unwilling to take my chances on sidesaddle riding. The motard began chatting with me.

"How do you know them?" the motard asked, glancing at Argentine and Mapendo's figures as they disappeared into the distance.

"They are my friends," I answered.

He grinned back at me. "Will you be my friend too?" he said with a wink.

"Well...I have a husband," I replied.

"Well then, perhaps you have a younger sister for me...one who can take me to live in America," he said as we pulled out into the crowded road.

"Well, there are a lot of very good women right here in Congo," I volleyed back at him. He chuckled and nodded his head in agreement.

When we slowed to a stop he twisted around on the motorcycle and continued our conversation.

"So how about your friends over there?" he said, nodding towards Argentine and Mapendo. "Are they married?" he asked.

"Nope. Not yet." I replied.

"Oh, they will never get married," he said dismissively. "I could never marry a disabled woman." He spoke in a tone that was still playful, unaware of my heart plummeting inside my chest.

Argentine and Mapendo were sliding down from their own motorcycles nearby, clicking their metal leg braces in place and grabbing their crutches. They couldn't quite hear our conversation. Argentine was laughing and joking with the young man who had driven her. She caught me looking at her and smiled and waved cheerfully. I knew that Mapendo and Argentine both wanted to get married. I knew it was an important part of their culture. And until that moment, I hadn't realized how unattainable that goal might be—how casually their dream might be dismissed.

I paid the motard and said goodbye quickly, no longer in the mood for his light-hearted conversation. As he drove away, I joined Argentine and Mapendo and tried to forget the conversation.

We had arrived at an open-air pavilion on the outskirts of town, a place I had never seen before, hidden just slightly behind some trees. I looked around and saw that the pavilion was surrounded by kingas parked outside. Men and women with physical disabilities from across Goma had put down their work and peddled in their kingas to arrive at this pavilion. It must have taken them hours just to arrive.

I found myself a seat on a bench and watched as Argentine and Mapendo sat down on the cement floor under the pavilion, throwing their crutches to the side, and unbuckling their metal leg braces. Their preparations for the game appeared to involve the exact opposite of most sports. Instead of putting equipment on, they were throwing it off, becoming more and more vulnerable.

The court looked like a volleyball court, with a net strung across the middle and teams on both sides. The only difference was that the net was at half height and all the players took their places on the ground, pulling themselves on the cement floor, their legs stretched out in front of them. This, I learned, was the game of *sitball.*

I sat there lost in thought, reminded of how Argentine was forced to move as a child, crawling on her hands and pulling her curled up legs behind her.

A referee blew the whistle, and the game began. Someone from the other team volleyed the ball over the net. Mapendo, in the front row, rushed into action, shifting her body three feet sideways and reaching an arm to block the ball. With a thud, she sent it back over the net. I marveled at the speed with which her arms had performed two separate functions, first scooting her body across the floor, and then shooting upward to block the ball.

I watched the rest of the game in fascination, realizing for the first time how strong Mapendo's upper body was. Next to me on the bench sat Bernadette and Berthe. They didn't play sitball, but they still they came out on their crutches to support their friends. I listened to their whoops and cheers and saw the excitement that ran across their faces. I couldn't help feeling that with each successful volley of the ball, they were all shrugging off a lifetime of stereotypes.

As the game carried on, I studied Mapendo's broad shoulders and her steady movements, and I noticed she was clearly the strongest player on the court. Argentine hit the ball less frequently, but her voice always rose up from the court. "Courage," she would call out in French, encouraging her team along. "Tunaweza. Tunaweza." "We can do this. We can do this."

CHAPTER THIRTY-THREE

The Website

Argentine and Mapendo continued sewing bags and purses every day. Bernadette also sewed, and Berthe often sat nearby, knitting baby clothing to sell in the market. I sat in that wooden house with my friends and watched Mapendo's foot bob up and down on the treadle. I saw Argentine standing at our large wooden table and cutting the cloth perfectly straight. There was a quiet sense of accomplishment and independence in that simple wooden house. I went to the photocopy vendors outside the university and printed paper tags with a SHONA logo on them. On the bottom of the tag I included a space for each woman to sign her name.

"For each of the bags that you sew, attach a tag, and then sign your name on the line," I told my friends, handing them blue Bic pens.

Argentine's eyes grew wide. "You do it for us!" she insisted. "Your handwriting is nicer!"

"Your handwriting is perfect," I told Argentine. I smiled every time I saw her careful, bubbly letters. Her handwriting was, in fact, better than mine. Argentine glanced at my face, then took the blue pen I was offering.

After a few months, I packed up the purses and bags in my suitcase for a trip to the United States to visit my parents. I sold almost everything I brought on that trip. "People bought the bags!" I reported to my friends on my return to Goma.

After that, I opened an account on eBay, trekking into my husband's office to use his internet connection over the weekend. I decided to try and sell a shirt with a reserve price of $20. It was a half-hearted experiment, and I was sure that no one would ever see our shirt, lost somewhere in the maze of eBay. I nearly fell over when I got an email telling me the shirt had sold to a customer in the United States.

"Oh no! How will I ship it?" I clutched my head in my hands.

In Goma, right near our house, was the old, colonial style post office. I had always assumed it to be entirely defunct. Between the volcano and Goma's exploding population, addresses no longer seemed to exist in Goma, and certainly I had never seen a mail carrier out delivering letters. However, like many things in Goma, it turned out that infrastructure had merely skipped a couple steps, leaping entirely over mailboxes and letter carriers, but offering international mail services such as DHL and EMS to people who could pay.

I shipped that first shirt for a hefty price through DHL. We didn't make a profit. But the customer left a glowing review and I began to see the possibilities. Still, we couldn't ship each single item through DHL. The cost would be overwhelming.

"Let me help you!" my mother said over the phone, offering to stock our purses in the United States and ship them for us as they sold on eBay. Soon, we were selling items regularly on eBay, and my mother was shipping them from her home in Connecticut.

After a while I realized that we needed a website. "You should learn HTML," my husband said, as though this might be easy. I downloaded a program that let me write code offline. I sat on my balcony, squinting at the screen in the sun, hoping my laptop battery would hold out, and learning how to make a website's font change color. That was our first website. It wasn't pretty, but it worked.

It was always a thrill to see a new customer on eBay or on our website. Every single person seemed like a miracle to me. *How did they find us?* I often asked myself, picturing Argentine, Mapendo, Berthe, Bernadette, and me sitting in that small wooden house in Goma.

CHAPTER THIRTY-FOUR

Blue and Orange Fabric

While Argentine, Mapendo and Bernadette would sew, I would go to the market to buy more cloth. Headed toward the fabric section, I would take a deep breath and walk straight through the meat section. I tried not to look at the tables buzzing with flies and meat, visceral and raw. Finally, I would reach the fabric section, a dimly lit maze with African cloth hung in overlapping rows on makeshift walls. The fabric muted the sound and light of the rest of the market. Walking into the cloth section felt like walking into a hushed library.

I loved looking at the vibrant colors of the fabric hanging on the walls. But I struggled with negotiating prices. I was always determined to get the "right price." I often prepared for the market by asking Argentine the exact prices of the fabric that she had purchased in the past. I arrived at the market with those prices stuck in my brain and fought doggedly to recreate them. In my mind, prices were a concrete thing. There was a right price and a wrong price.

The first time I went to buy fabric, I picked out a brilliant blue fabric with orange flower designs from one of the vendors.

"Ni nzuri sana." "It's very nice," the vendor said, pulling down the cloth.

"Bei gani?" I asked. "What price is it?"

"Nipe vingt," she said. "Give me twenty."

"Hapana. Ile haiko bei." "No, that is not the price." I responded, my cheeks growing warm.

The woman raised her eyebrows and chuckled. She lowered the price a dollar, still smiling.

My face grew red. "Dix-sept," I said firmly. "Seventeen." That was the price Argentine told me she bought her cloth for.

By this time, I knew how to bargain in the market. I knew that simply stating my end price was not bargaining.

But knowing something and accepting it are two different things. With this fabric negotiation, I felt like my whole identity was on the line. I wanted to show that I knew the "correct" price of things, that I wasn't just a foolish foreigner willing to pay any price. I wanted to show that I was a local, that Goma was my home.

"Dix-sept" I insisted again, keeping my voice low and steady.

The vendor shook her head and lifted her eyebrows in mock surprise. To her, this was all theater.

But then I went off script.

"Acha."—"Leave it," I said, spinning on my heel angrily and walking away.

I went home without the blue and orange fabric that day. I don't think I convinced anyone that Goma was my home, not even myself.

CHAPTER THIRTY-FIVE

Prices

It took me a long time to get used to buying fabric at the market. I could never quite shake my American conviction that everything should have a "correct" price, preferably written on a little white sticker.

But I started to stand in the shadows, beneath the brightly colored fabric, and watch other customers. I saw how Congolese women approached the vendors, bantering prices back and forth, chatting with them for what seemed like an eternity to me. I saw how the banter was like water to these market vendors. It provided a break in the monotony of a long, slow market day. I also came to realize that the banter served a purpose. These customers and vendors were learning little facts about each other's lives. I was so busy trying to protect myself from being cheated out of a dollar that I was cheating us all out of so much more.

Finally, I learned to go to the market, not for one hour, but for several. I learned to let my "correct price" sit in the back of my head and never speak it. Instead, I started chatting in Swahili, inquiring after children, throwing prices back and forth like a ball, and leaning my head back to laugh. My slow conversations and casual banter didn't always bring me the best price. But somehow, I no longer cared so much.

When I brought the cloth back to Argentine and Mapendo, they always congratulated me, as though I had chosen the best possible cloth. They never asked about the exact price I had paid, instead they rubbed the cloth between their thumbs and forefingers, feeling the weight of it. They opened the yards of cloth and inspected it for misprints. And finally, they began to cut.

CHAPTER THIRTY-SIX

Mothers

My mother came to visit us in Goma. She had never been to Africa before, and her friends looked at her skeptically when she said she was going to the Democratic Republic of Congo. But I am an only child and when I got married, I remember the fierce look in my mother's eyes. She knew that my husband had grown up in Africa. She had heard him talk about the fishing boats on Lake Kivu, the sound of the birds in the morning, and the smell of night-blooming jasmine. I don't think she was surprised when we first announced that we would be moving back to the region for a while. "Don't you worry," she whispered to me grabbing my hand, "I'll come wherever you go."

I remember my mother's wide eyes when I put her on a motorcycle taxi that first time, instructing her to sit on the back and hold onto the driver with both hands. She was well into her sixties at the time—perhaps I should have reconsidered the motorcycle taxi, but it was one of my favorite ways to experience Goma. My mother loved bicycles, and I was sure she would love motorcycles too.

When we arrived at the market, the cloth vendors called out to us from far away, "Ohhh...this is your mother!!!"

"She hasn't gotten old at all yet," one woman said.

"A mzungu never gets old!" another vendor declared authoritatively.

Everyone loved meeting my mother. In Goma there were plenty of foreigners. There were the Indian soldiers with the MONUC tanks. There were expats who arrived to work with aid or development programs. There was even a night club scene. But foreigners rarely arrived with children in tow, never mind parents.

I think of it now and realize how strangely disembodied we foreigners must have seemed. In Congo, family defines so much of a person's identity. And here we were, like aliens floating down from the sky, no family in sight.

Of course, I did have my husband, but even that had proven to be a sticking point with my Congolese friends. Most of my Congolese friends used the word *bwana* to refer to their husbands. But the actual translation of bwana is "master" or "boss." I staunchly refused to refer to my husband as "bwana." I replaced *bwana* with *mume,* another Swahili word for husband, less commonly used in Goma. To my ears, the two words for husband had a different ring. But to my friend's ears, "He's not my husband! He's my *husband,*" is all they heard.

They nodded politely and probably decided that my marriage was entirely unfathomable.

So, when my mother arrived, my friends were delighted. The cloth vendors fawned over my mother, with her big blue eyes that matched mine, delighting in our resemblance.

"She's your mother!" they would declare even before I introduced her. "The mzungu has brought her mother," they shouted enthusiastically, following their declaration with applause and hugs. This, finally, was a relationship everyone could understand.

I took my mother to meet Argentine and Mapendo. "This is my mother," I said when I brought her by the house.

They smiled their approval. "Ndiyo, dada," they replied. "Yes, sister."

"Aren't you surprised by how far she has come?" I asked them.

"Oh no, we're not surprised, "they answered. "We knew she would come. She's your mother."

CHAPTER THIRTY-SEVEN

Water

Running water arrived in our apartment only sporadically. Every week or two, the pipes would rattle in the night, pulling us from our dreams. "Grab the hose!" my husband would shout.

We would rush into the kitchen with a black hose in our hands, still blurry from sleep. Then we would hurriedly attach one end of the hose to the kitchen faucet and run the other end into a large water barrel that sat in the corner of our little kitchen.

Finally, we would sit, listening to the miraculous sounds of running water and waiting for our barrel to fill.

During the day, our faucets were usually dry. I learned to dip water from the water barrel and carry it carefully to the bathroom to wash my body. I dipped water from the barrel to wash dishes, to cook, and to clean.

But, this was a luxury compared to the reality for most of the residents of Goma. Most people lived in small structures with no plumbing at all. Instead of waiting for the whooshing of water at night, they sent young girls to the lake or to pumps across town. The girls would return carrying the water back home in yellow jugs on the tops of their heads or draped down their backs. I saw them in the streets each day, little girls no more than six or seven years old carrying giant containers of water. Sometimes they laughed and chatted as they walked, but when I looked in their little-girl eyes, I could see the weight of all that they carried.

CHAPTER THIRTY-EIGHT

Electricity

Our apartment also had electricity which arrived occasionally. It arrived more regularly than the water, but usually stayed for only a couple of hours at a time. In Goma, I learned to walk into a room and listen for the hum of electricity, something I had never noticed before.

Sometimes, I enjoyed not having electricity in the evenings. I liked the way it slowed life down. In our hyper-lit world of New York City, I had rarely laid down my work at dusk, but in Goma—without electricity—the evening brought rest.

Still, I have always liked a good TV show at the end of the day. I often begged my husband to bring home his laptop fully charged from his office so that we could huddle around it, the blue screen lighting our faces.

We had no internet in our apartment, but our street was lined with little shops selling bootleg DVDs. Sometimes, after a DVD run, I returned triumphantly to the apartment with a popular new American movie, only to discover it was dubbed into French, my disappointment written all over my face. Other times, the DVDs featured muffled voices and the strange sounds of coughing in the middle of important romance scenes. Then there were the times that a movie would cut off midway through, a cliff hanger the director had never intended. It was always a gamble.

At some point, I stumbled on a trove of DVDs with episode after episode of the series *24*. This frenetic, adrenaline-pumping show featured Jack Bauer leading a counter-terrorism unit. The program was filled with violence and a heavy-handed insistence that somehow America was always in the right. I, in my New York apartment, would have turned my nose up, demanding a show that fit my politics. But this was Congo, and *24* was in English, with no dubbing, and there was a pile of disks that we could work through season by season. I was hooked.

One night, the electricity was out, and my husband and I were sitting on our couch, watching *24* on his laptop, when my husband's phone rang.

I heard his gruff answers, and then silence as he clicked off his phone. There had been a shooting. Dieu Donné had been killed in his home. Dieu Donné was a guard who worked at my husband's office, the same guard who had worked at our first house, with his soft-spoken nature, smiling quietly at my attempts at dinnertime conversations. Dieu Donné had been working hard to build his large family a house. He had taken a loan to buy a plot of land on the outskirts of town. I had finally learned I could tempt him into conversation by asking about the house. His face would light up as he described pouring the concrete floor. "We added a new room!" he would proudly report, or "We put up the metal roof today."

Then one day he had straightened his back and looked me right in my eye. "My family moved into the house last week," he announced with his chest puffed up.

Shortly after Dieu Donné and his family moved into their house on the outskirts of town, armed men broke in during the night. They took Dieu Donné outside and shot him. The bullet passed through his chest and pierced the newly constructed wooden house where his wife and children huddled inside.

My husband and I sat in silence at the news.

I must have said something to my husband that night. But all I remember is that after a while I wanted to distract us from darkness. I hit play on my husband's laptop, thinking perhaps we could continue the show we'd been watching. After only a few seconds, gunshots exploded from the screen, Jack Bauer bravely dodging bullet after bullet—an American hero who never got hit. My generally unflappable husband turned and looked at me grimly. "I can't watch this right now," he said.

I turned the program off and never had the stomach to turn it on again.

We never learned why Dieu Donné was killed. Some people reported that the armed men who broke into his house had asked each other "Is this him?" Rumors multiplied, as they always do, to fill in the void left by inexplicable tragedy.

Dieu Donné's death was the second death in a month. A few weeks earlier, another of my husband's coworkers had been killed. The two deaths could have been unrelated. They probably were. Or perhaps they weren't. In Goma, tragedies often seem to fall one on top of another, leaving only suspicion and fear in their wake. The months after my husband's coworkers died were dark. We waited, always, for another phone call, another disaster.

But life continued. Goma has the unimaginable ability to pile tragedy upon tragedy, and then, in the very next moment, return to the sensation of normal. Like a weeble-wobble toy determined to right itself, life in Goma continued in the face of every catastrophe.

CHAPTER THIRTY-NINE

The Air in Goma

Sometimes on my way to the market, I would walk down the main road and suddenly notice that even though it was the middle of the day, the shoe vendors had already packed up their glittery high heels. I'd glance around and see the tailors hurriedly pulling their sewing machines back inside and shutting their wooden doors. The streets would start emptying out as though a storm was coming, and I would stand there, glancing at the brilliant blue sky in confusion.

Everything in Goma can change in an instant. From time to time, my phone would ring with a call from my husband, telling me to get home as soon as I could. Sometimes it was because of a riot in town. Other times it was because gunfire had been heard in the distance and there was growing alarm that the rebel soldiers who operated in the rural areas surrounding the city might be preparing an attack. Upon reports that rebels had taken areas nearby, the market would suddenly shut down. Shops would close in fear of looting, and everyone would rush home to hunker down behind locked doors. Sometimes it was a false alarm, like the time a soldier in Birere had accidentally discharged his weapon. No one was hurt, but it sent the entire city into lockdown as rumors of an attack circulated.

Other times it wasn't a false alarm. In the weeks leading up to October of 2008, Nkunda's CNDP rebels had been advancing on the city of Goma, taking one key position after another. News filtered into Goma. "The rebels took Mweso," they said one day. A few weeks later they said, "The rebels took Rumangabo." With each update, the rebels were drawing closer to Goma.

CHAPTER FORTY

Throwing Stones

October 2008

One day, I was sitting in the wooden house with Argentine, Mapendo, Berthe, and Bernadette. I had just come from the cloth market with piles of new African fabric and we were in the middle of a meeting, staring down at brilliant yellow and blue cloth.

"Let's sew tote bags with this cloth," I suggested in Swahili.

"Dada, don't you think this cloth would be better for a skirt?" Argentine pointed out. I nodded in agreement. I loved talking about cloth. I loved the way my friends would weigh in with their own strong opinions. I wished all of life would divide out so evenly.

Suddenly we heard a popping sound in the air. It sounded like gunshots coming from nearby Birere, where my apartment was. We looked at each other, then looked at the flimsy wooden walls surrounding us. We huddled closer together.

I called my husband who was at his office in Birere.

"People are throwing rocks at MONUC soldiers," he said. "Those gunshots were probably MONUC soldiers firing in the air, trying to disperse the crowds."

I understood why the people of Goma were frustrated. Every day there were new reports of their own government soldiers abandoning positions and running toward Goma in a panic before the rebels even arrived. The government soldiers were generally poorly paid, poorly equipped, and poorly trained. No one was surprised that they ran. But then there was MONUC, with their blue helmets and their heavy equipment. "Where was MONUC?" the people of Goma began to ask. "What were all these soldiers in their blue helmets doing?"

Sitting in Argentine and Mapendo's wooden house, I could hear the forced calm in my husband's voice over the phone. "Get home as quickly as you can," he said.

On my way walk home, the air was electric. Cars rushed down back roads. Motorcycles sped by. Parents were sending motards to pick up children from school before conditions deteriorated further. Shops hurriedly locked their doors in fear of pillaging.

I got home and waited. Soon my husband called again. "Grab your passport. We have to go," he said. "I'll be there with a car in a minute."

We rarely traveled by car. We walked or took motorcycle taxis almost everywhere we went. When my husband said he was bringing a car, I knew that something was wrong, something requiring rolled-up windows—hardened glass between us and the rest of the world. The city looked different that day from my high perch in an SUV. I stared out my window at the peanut vendors and money changers that I usually walked by and greeted by name.

At the border we held our breath, always waiting for a problem with our passports, never quite sure if they would let us out of Congo and into Rwanda. Borders are a funny thing. They were often relatively easy to cross with our American passports, but at every crossing we were reminded that we were visitors in someone else's country. We crossed at the pleasure of those in power and the whim of the officials waving us through.

In just a few minutes we were waved across, and my husband and I found ourselves standing awkwardly on a dusty Rwandan road, adrenaline still pumping. *Now what?* We wondered.

We found a local guesthouse nearby, a few steps from the border, so close that we could see Congo from our window. Immediately, my husband was on the phone trying to find out more details about what was happening.

Goma was in a panic. As fear of a rebel invasion grew, angry crowds had attacked a MONUC convoy that was evacuating United Nations civilian staff. The crowd had thrown large rocks at the windows. There were reports that a motard had also been accidentally killed by a MONUC vehicle. There was chaos in the streets, and anger at foreigners.

That night we barely slept. We lay in our beds listening to the sounds of gunfire just across the border. My heart sank. *What was happening to all my friends?*

No one knew what was going on, most certainly not the people of Goma, who were locked up in their houses. Our phones beeped with messages from Goma. My husband's coworkers described what they heard going on in the darkness, the sounds of gunfire followed by shouting. *Were the rebels attacking Goma?* Argentine and Mapendo sent me texts saying they had locked the door, barricaded it as best they could. "Mungu akulinde." "God protect you," they messaged me.

How could I respond to that? I was safe. I had disappeared across the border in less than half an hour. Mapendo and Argentine, along with Berthe and Bernadette, with their crutches and leg braces, were trapped in a wooden house with a door that would never hold up. It was true that I was a foreigner in Congo, and, in this particular chaos, I might have been a target, a symbol of the international community which has failed Congo for so long. But, in the unpredictability of Goma, who was to say that Argentine and Mapendo wouldn't become targets also?

That gut-wrenching night stretched on forever.

The next morning my husband and I awoke at our hotel. We went down for breakfast and sat at a white plastic table, trying to swallow buttery eggs and soft white bread. Dotted across the front yard were other plastic tables, with other expats who had fled from Goma. Everyone was checking their phones and talking in whispers.

A kilometer away, in Goma, shops remained shuttered, and the streets were strangely quiet. The population was still hunkering behind locked doors, unsure what had happened the previous night.

Gradually the news trickled out. To everyone's surprise, the rebels had not taken Goma. They had reached the outskirts of the city and stopped short. The shooting we had heard during the night had been from chaos of another kind. More than two hundred prisoners in the central prison in Goma had rioted. The guards had lost control, and the prisoners poured out into surrounding neighborhoods. Shooting exploded through the night from the guards trying to keep control of the prison and recapture escaped prisoners.

No one was sure what would happen next in Goma. The rebels were still just north of the city and the city was collectively holding its breath.

I called Argentine and Mapendo. They had listened to the shooting all night, frozen in fear. "Uwende mbiyo. Uvuke frontière," I said. "Go quickly. Cross the border." I didn't know what would happen next, but I was unwilling to spend another night wondering if they were okay on the other side of an invisible line.

"Ndiyo, dada," Mapendo said, her usually steady voice, trembling slightly in relief.

"Ndoja! Ngoja!"—"Wait! Wait!" I called out just before she clicked off the phone. "Pack the purple dress!"

I stood outside the hotel that morning and waited, my heart stuck in my throat. I didn't know if they would be able to get across the border. Finally, Argentine appeared in the distance, swinging both legs forward with each step. Behind her, I could see Mapendo and Bernadette and Berthe. We hugged and I took them to a guest house nearby.

During the next few days, Goma spiraled further into crisis. In the face of the rebel approach, government forces who had been stationed north of the city had fallen into disarray and began to abandon their positions en masse. Even in better times, the government troops were known for quickly abandoning positions. Now they were in a panic and the only way to retreat was through Goma. These soldiers hit Goma in complete disorder, tanks roaring toward town as they fled west. They stole cars and motorcycles from the local population. They waved their guns and shot in the air, a facade of bravado to cover the shame of retreat. Over the next several nights the panicked soldiers began pillaging homes, looting shops, extorting families, and raping women. Commanders appeared to have lost control of their retreating troops, or they had abandoned them altogether.

Suddenly Goma fell into a power vacuum, and it was unclear who was in control of the city, if anyone. The government soldiers had abandoned Goma, assuming the rebel soldiers were taking control. But the rebel troops stopped just short of the city limits, perhaps to accentuate the government chaos and the rebel restraint. Goma was left in a void. The Congolese government brought in a new commander with a heavy hand, bent on restoring some measure of order to the city. His units began shooting looters on the spot, but many of those looters were government soldiers themselves, creating a strange alternate reality where government soldiers were shooting at themselves. From our neighbors we heard that a drunk and belligerent soldier had arrived at the trucking compound where we lived, intent on pillaging the compound. A police officer was summoned and, when the police officer arrived, he promptly shot and killed the unruly government soldier.

Eventually the rebel forces declared a unilateral ceasefire from their position at the outskirts of town. They called on MONUC forces to restore order in Goma. As it became clear that the rebels were not taking control, government troops who had fled through the city began to return.

We followed all these developments from just over the border in Rwanda. Each day we wondered when it would be safe enough to return to Goma. The city was on edge, but my husband needed to return for work. By the end of the week, we had decided to return to our apartment in the trucking compound. I remember crossing the border into Congo, the same border I had crossed the first time a few years before. This time, Congo felt strangely subdued, as though there was a blanket over the place. Shortly afterwards, Berthe and Bernadette went back to live with their families in Goma. For a while Bernadette tried to continue sewing SHONA bags from her family home, but she found it difficult to work from home and eventually she moved on to other work. Berthe continued to knit baby clothes from her home and sell them in the market. Meanwhile Argentine and Mapendo stayed in Rwanda for several more months. I helped them rent a small house in Rwanda and they kept sewing

SHONA bags and purses from there, waiting for Congo to stabilize enough to return.

CHAPTER FORTY-ONE

The Purple Dress

One of our first customers on eBay was a woman named Lynn. She sang in the Chicago Mass Choir and she needed to buy a custom-made African dress to wear with her choir. The whole choir had been asked to purchase African dresses. I imagined most of the choir members had found an African seamstress in Chicago to sew an outfit for them. But somehow Lynn had found us on the other side of the world.

Lynn chose a lovely fabric, deep purple with tiny golden flowers, and she asked us to sew her a boubou-style dress. Lynn had also told the other choir members about her purchase. "There are these women with disabilities in eastern Congo. They sew dresses and sell them on eBay."

The story had sounded too good to be true. "Let us know when you get that dress," the other choir members said with a laugh.

Mapendo had finished sewing that dress for Lynn just before Goma fell apart. "Wait! Wait!" I had called out. "Pack the purple dress!" And Mapendo did. She crossed the border to safety with a purple dress tucked in her bag.

I sent an email to Lynn to explain the situation. *The SHONA Congo women have had to flee across the border because rebels are threatening to take control of the city,* I emailed. *But don't worry! We brought your dress, and we will mail it from Rwanda. Thank you for being our customer!*

Lynn must have wondered whether this dress would ever arrive. We looked like an internet scam, with promises of African dresses that were strangely delayed by the war. But Lynn held out hope and waited for her SHONA dress.

These were the kind of customers we had—the kind of customers we still have today. They are people who go out of their way to find us and to believe in us.

Lynn's dress arrived just on time. She wore it to her choir concert and sent us a picture. She also sent us a Chicago Mass Choir CD. Argentine listened to those gospel songs. They were in a language she didn't know, but still she seemed to understand them exactly.

CHAPTER FORTY-TWO

Climbing the Stairs

February 2009

When Argentine and Mapendo finally returned to Congo, they came to live at my apartment. Goma was still tense, and we were all too scared to return them to their own house, with its flimsy wooden door.

My second-floor apartment sat at the top of a long flight of cement stairs. When Argentine and Mapendo first arrived in the trucking compound, crutches under their arms, they squinted upward, their faces unreadable.

"Should we get someone to carry you?" I asked.

"Tunaweza," Argentine replied, always confident. "We can do it."

Argentine stood at the base of the stairs, a tiny figure staring upward. Then she placed both crutches on the first stair in front of her. Lifting herself onto her crutches, she threw her legs forward. The movement appeared to consist of sheer willpower. People in the trucking compound stopped to watch, but Argentine just kept facing forward, moving up one step at a time. Mapendo did the same.

When they got to the top of the stairs, they greeted my neighbors and then turned to look out over the balcony.

Argentine stared off into the distance, standing higher than she ever had before. "Look," she said pointing off to the right. I saw nothing but the green hills that stretched out before me every day. "You can see Rwanda from here. That there is the border," Argentine said.

I squinted off into the distance, where the lines of houses gradually faded into green hills. Still I saw nothing. To me, it seemed impossible to find that magic line that had offered us protection—that line where one country ended, and another began.

CHAPTER FORTY-THREE

Smoked Fish

Argentine and Mapendo lived with my husband and me for several months. During the day they would cut cloth and sew. At night, when the electricity would go off, we would eat by candlelight, the four us gathered around a coffee table. Argentine talked about growing up in Masisi. My husband told stories from his childhood in Rwanda and Burundi. There was a richness and a simplicity to that time. It reminded me of gathering under a tin roof while the rain pounded hard outside. We formed a community that lasted even after the rain had stopped.

Eventually Goma felt calm enough that Argentine and Mapendo returned to live in their own wooden house. Before they moved back home, they decided to surprise me with a meal that they had cooked themselves. While I was out in the market, they cooked smoked fish in a red sauce.

All my life I have hated eating fish. When I was a child, my mother served fish on Fridays, and I developed a strong distaste for Fridays. Up until this point, I had managed to politely avoid the smoked fish in Goma. For starters, the smoked fish wasn't from Goma, or from Lake Kivu at all. Rather it traveled the bumpy roads of Congo from somewhere upcountry. By the time it arrived in Goma, it had sat out for weeks on the flat beds of trucks or on wooden carts. It was then hung in market stalls, brown and shriveled looking.

When I returned home from the market that day, weighed down with African fabric, Argentine and Mapendo grinned at me. "Dada, tukule pa moja." "Sister, let's eat together," Mapendo said to me.

Argentine and Mapendo had cooked the smoked fish whole and it lay in the red sauce, empty eyes staring up at us beneath the tomato and onion. Argentine prayed over the food. She thanked God for our safety and thanked God for the smoked fish. "Amen!" she declared.

Mapendo dug into the skin of the fish, selecting out morsels of meat, removing bones from her mouth as she chewed. Then she moved onto the head of the fish. "The head is Mapendo's favorite part," Argentine said, as though they had lived together all their lives.

"Dada, hautakula?" "Sister, aren't you going to eat?" Mapendo asked me, pointedly, glancing at my hand, still settled on my lap. "Here is some good meat," she said, pointing in the direction of the middle of the fish.

I lifted my hand and sunk my fingers into the flesh of the fish. I plucked out little chunks of meat, with Argentine and Mapendo laughing at my timid attempts to separate the flesh from the bone. After the first bite, I discovered that it was delicious.

CHAPTER FORTY-FOUR

Partners

Argentine and Mapendo and I decided that we needed a few more sewing partners. It was nearly the end of the school year, and a new group of young women was preparing to graduate from the sewing program at the Centre pour Handicapés. Argentine and Mapendo knew two of the women, Riziki and Solange. They were from rural villages and were likely to struggle after they graduated from the Center, unable to return to their villages because of safety concerns. We asked them if they would like to sew with SHONA, and they happily agreed, moving into that wooden house with Argentine and Mapendo.

Although Riziki and Solange had learned to sew at the Center, we knew that they would need training for sewing with SHONA. I bought poster board from a shop downtown. "Oh good, you are going to teach them lessons," Argentine said touching my arm and nodding approvingly.

"No, *you* are going to teach the lessons," I said back to her, gesturing toward both Argentine and Mapendo.

"Oh nooooo...we've never been to school. We can't do that!" Argentine replied.

Argentine and Mapendo spent days preparing.

"We should talk about quality control, and about helping each other, and about why we can't use cheap zippers." Argentine said.

Then, in bubbly writing that slanted upward, they spelled out the values of their lives—the steadiness, hard work and generosity that I had watched them live out over the previous two years.

Riziki and Solange came to my apartment for the workshops led by Argentine and Mapendo. They climbed my stairs on crutches just as Argentine and Mapendo had. Then they sat on my couch in the living room, looking nervous and excited, blue ballpoint pens poised carefully above their square ruled notebooks. Argentine stood up to lead the first workshop, leaning on the wooden crutches under her arms. I had hung her poster board on my living room wall, but it was too high up, and with her small frame she could barely point to her own bubbly writing. But it didn't matter. She didn't really need to see her outline anyway. Puffed up ten feet tall, with her voice booming across the room, Argentine shrugged off every doubt she had mentioned just a few days earlier.

"We have to sew really, really carefully," Argentine explained confidently to the new recruits. "We send our bags to America," she said pausing and looking around meaningfully.

For a minute I was distracted, wondering what America looked like in Argentine's head. Trying to combat Hollywood stereotypes, I'd explained the history of slavery in the United States and our nation's crimes against indigenous people. I had explained the fight for civil rights. We'd talked about Frederick Douglas and Rosa Parks. But now it seemed Argentine was more focused on something else I had said about America.

"In America, not many people know how to sew! There aren't even a lot of sewing shops!" Argentine declared, her voice half disbelief and half amusement. “If a seam rips open on one of our bags, a lot of people won’t know how to fix it. They’ll just throw our bag out,” Argentine concluded with a look of horror on her face.

Riziki and Solange nodded solemnly and wrote down every word.

CHAPTER FORTY-FIVE

Leaving

July 2009

Three years had soon passed, and my husband and I began to prepare to return to the United States. When we moved to Congo, we had committed to three years. Over the three years, I had talked to my parents often on the phone. I flew back to visit them, and they came out to visit me. But I knew the toll that the distance had taken. I wanted to live closer to my parents, but I also had fallen in love with Goma. Now our time was over too fast.

My husband's coworkers held a goodbye party for us. Only three years earlier, they had held a welcome party. At the goodbye party, my husband's coworkers sat in a circle, singing songs in Swahili. They stood up one after another to give generous speeches in Swahili, French, and English. I swallowed hard, hoping to dislodge the lump in my throat. It seemed so unfair. We had been the guests, and I was sure that I had gained far more than I had given. But no one held parties to celebrate the people who stayed behind. No one held celebrations for all the people who made Congo what I loved, the boys who had sold me peanuts, the motards who had carried me safely over the years, or the finely dressed Congolese women who held their heads high through streets of lava rock. I had spent three years fighting to be part of Goma, to find some path toward community—toward justice and equality. But in the end, I was doing exactly what very few of them could do. I was leaving. In that moment, I ran up against a truth that for three years had escaped me—my privilege to come and to go, to cross borders and then to make my way home, was more precious than any of the fancy houses that I could have rented. It was a privilege that I had taken too lightly.

On our final day in Congo, I invited Argentine, Mapendo, Riziki, and Solange to cross over the border to Rwanda with me. "Unisindikize," I said. *Sindikiza* means to accompany someone part of the way home. In Congo, I had learned to always sindikiza my guests. I would accompany them down our steps and out of the trucking compound, walking with them for a couple minutes before our ways parted.

This time it was my friends' turn to sindikiza me.

We crossed the border into Rwanda, the chaos of Congo receding into the distance. Slowly, with my friends on crutches, we walked to a beautiful restaurant on the shore of Lake Kivu. At the restaurant, we sat in white plastic chairs on the green grass, staring at the sparkling water. Argentine and Mapendo told stories about one time when they had competed in a sitball competition on the other side of the lake. "We took these tiny boats across the lake. I was sure we would tip over, and I would drown," Argentine said, laughing.

"Mungu wangu," Mapendo said with her eyes wide. "Ilikuwa hatari." "My God. It was so dangerous." And then Argentine and Mapendo looked at each other, the fear still playing in their minds. They glanced back at the water, dark and mysterious underneath the sparkles. Then they looked at their own feet, buckled into metal leg braces. They shook their heads, as though dislodging the memory.

"Oh yes, I was soooo afraid," Argentine said, reaching an arm out to Mapendo. Together, they collapsed into laughter.

On the day I left Goma, I had no idea what lay in store for my friends. But I knew that life in Goma was precarious at best. I hugged my friends goodbye, knowing that I couldn't protect them from any of it.

"Usitusahau," they said as they grabbed onto me. "Don't forget us."

And then they let go.

I left, promising myself that I would return soon. It would be nine years before I would see my friends again.

Part II

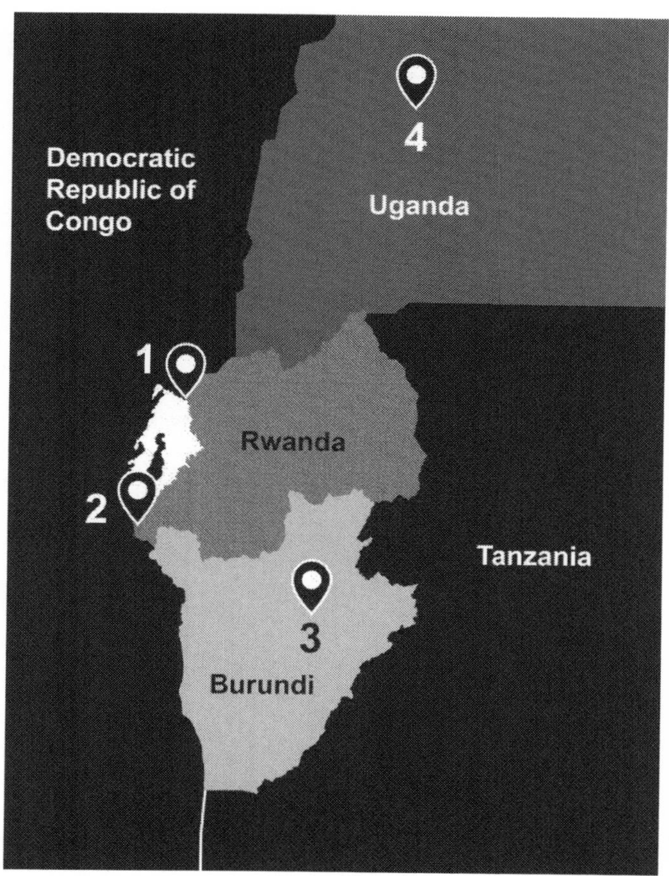

1 Goma

2 Bukavu

3 Ruyigi Refugee Camp

4 Rwamwanja Refugee Camp

*white area represents Lake Kivu

CHAPTER FORTY-SIX

Worried

August 2009

When I left Goma, I worried that my Swahili wouldn't be good enough to carry my friendships over long distance phone lines. I feared that what I could communicate in person, face to face, with the aid of gestures and context, would fall flat over phone lines. "Sitakusahau." "I will not forget you," I had promised, while nervously conducting practice phone conversations in Swahili.

Now, I sat in an apartment in New York, trying to follow Mapendo's phone calls.

"Sema pole pole!"—"Speak slowly!" I urged Mapendo as she soared through conversations with her understated style.

"Ngoja!" "Wait!" I stopped her mid-sentence. "What did you just say? Did you say that your brother-in-law died?"

"Ndiyo, dada," she answered in a calm, steady voice. "Yes, sister."

My question broke her train of thought and she paused for a moment. Then she picked up the threads to her story again, words spilling out at a rapid pace. I closed my eyes and tried to concentrate, tuning out the sounds of New York City outside my window.

After a few more minutes, I interrupted again, “Wait, wait,” I said, in a slightly panicked tone. “Is this your sister’s husband, the one who lives in Goma with eight children?”

“Yes, yes,” she replied, “although she also takes care of two orphans, so it is really ten children.”

“Neema’s father?” my voice rose up. “You mean Neema’s father has died?” I asked, remembering Neema, Mapendo’s sweet little niece, cooking beans at the charcoal stove while Mapendo sewed.

“Yes, her father,” Mapendo answered, then continued, “I don’t know how my sister will take care of all the kids. Maybe Neema’s younger sister, Ziada, will come to live with us also,” Mapendo said, her voice trailing off.

“How did he die?” I broke in between Mapendo’s words.

“We don’t know,” Mapendo responded with a voice that lilted upward just slightly, a question mark on the end of her statement. “He just died. He wasn’t sick at all . . . maybe someone poisoned him.” Her words carried Congo back to me—the inexplicable tragedies that gave birth to suspicions, the open-ended questions with no answer at all.

“Pole sana,” I said to Mapendo. “I am sorry.”

Finally, I understood this conversation that we had been having for the past hour. Hidden in the midst of Mapendo’s steady voice, and the words that I couldn’t quite understand, I had caught sight of the family tragedy that had just taken place—a father ripped from his children, a mother left on her own—a replay of Mapendo’s own childhood tragedy.

“People are trying to take the house away from my sister. She will have nothing,” Mapendo said, referring to the small home that Mapendo’s sister and her husband had owned. It was the same brutal struggle for resources that I had seen facing other widows in Goma, the compounding of loss upon loss.

I sat there holding the phone, tangled in my own thoughts about Congo and tragedy and the overwhelming forces that seem to make it impossible for the poor to rise. After a few minutes, I realized that Mapendo was still talking. I concentrated again on her words again. "We'll send you the bags tomorrow," she concluded. She had jumped directly from tragedy to survival. She was going to send me some bags.

CHAPTER FORTY-SEVEN

Inside the Box

I gave Mapendo my new address in Brooklyn. "Make sure you check the bags very carefully before you send them to me," I said in Swahili, my voice betraying my nervousness.

Sewing in Congo had an impermanent air. Dresses were always being adjusted, styles were changed, and stitches were replaced. But with me in New York now, everything had to be right the first time. It was a risk.

"Dada, do you really think we can do it?" Argentine had asked me before I left.

Mapendo had responded before I could open my mouth. "Ndiyo. Tutaweza." she'd said. "Yes, we will be able."

But none of us really knew. The bags might have mistakes. Or the colors of the cloth might not be sellable. My address could be wrong. The bags could be held indefinitely in customs.

Before I had left, one of the cloth vendors had asked what my friends would do after I left Goma.

"They'll keep sewing," I had blurted out quickly.

"Oh no," the vendor had exclaimed. "They need someone to manage the project—to buy the cloth, to ship the bags, to divide up the money."

"They can do it themselves," I had answered, willing it to be true. I had seen many projects fail in Goma during my three years there. And I was busy planning for disaster. I thought that if each of my friends could buy their own cloth, ship their own bags, and receive their own money, they could keep going no matter what happened.

But now, I wondered whether this direction had been the right choice. I pictured Mapendo, balanced sideways on a motorcycle carrying her crutches in one arm and her bundle of forty-six SHONA bags in the other. What if she fell over backward?

Mapendo didn't fall over backward. She made it to the post office that day. Three weeks later, I found a small yellow paper in my mailbox. It was a notice of a package held at the post office. I swallowed hard, my heart racing as I walked to the post office to pick up the package.

I arrived at the post office and joined the long line that snaked in circles around the small building. Finally, I stepped up to the window. The clerk, an older lady with glasses and greying hair, peered at my package notification and then disappeared frowning into another room. Eventually, she returned shaking her head.

"Too big. Too heavy," she said, with arms stretched wide, glancing skeptically at the folding grocery cart I had brought along.

"It's okay. I can do it," I promised her.

She shook her head and went back to the other room, then reemerged pushing a cardboard box on the floor. "Forty-four pounds (twenty kilograms)," she said, disapprovingly. Forty-four pounds was the weight limit for this type of package.

The clerk motioned to a side door and then pushed the package on the floor out the door. "Good luck," she said.

The package didn't fit in the folding grocery cart that I had brought, so I balanced it precariously on top, gingerly pushing the cart forward. Every time I pushed, the cart moved forward a bit, and then the box threatened to topple off the cart. I placed one hand on the package and the other hand on the handle of the cart and pushed forward again, trying to keep my balance. I walked the twelve blocks home, pushing the cart with one hand, wondering whether the bags that were inside would be bags that I could sell. At the first curb, I eased the cart gently down and then up again. The package toppled onto the sidewalk strewn with bubblegum stains.

"Hakuna shida," I told myself. "No problem." I imagined how much more difficult Mapendo's journey to the post office in Goma must have been.

Eventually I got the package home. I carried it up two flights of stairs to our third-floor apartment. Then I found a knife and cut open the yellow tape. The smell of charcoal floated into the air. I reached inside the box and pulled out neatly folded stacks of bags, brilliantly colored and carefully sewn. I stacked the bags in piles on my floor, sorting for color and style, stopping to inspect the fabric from time to time. *Tutaweza,* I thought to myself. *We can do this.*

In the bottom of the box, my hand touched something that seemed to move. I jumped back, then peered in from the top of the box. It was a large plastic bag filled with uncooked rice, the kind sold at the market in Goma, still studded with small stones. With it came a handwritten note.

Dada, tunakukumbuka.

Sister we are remembering you.

In her bubbly writing, Argentine had signed her name.

My mind flashed back to my latest conversation with Argentine. I had been trying to tell her that I didn't have much extra money to send to Congo because I hadn't found a job yet in New York, and life was expensive. "It's not easy here," I had probably said.

Argentine sent me a kilogram of rice, as though I were her neighbor living just next door.

When I factored in our international shipping costs, that was the most expensive bag of rice I have ever possessed. But the gesture filled my heart with a strange type of gratitude. Half a world away, Argentine had packed a bag of rice into a cardboard box, treating me just like her neighbor next door. Without knowing it, she had given me exactly what I had always been looking for.

CHAPTER FORTY-EIGHT

Always a Foreigner

Sometimes Argentine asked me about New York. "What is it like?" But I had no Swahili words that could describe my new neighborhood in Brooklyn where women sold tamales out of grocery carts on our sidewalk and elderly Chinese men practiced tai chi in the park. It was a neighborhood where every person I met came from somewhere else. And that made me feel at home.

There is something about having lived as a foreigner. It changes you. While I lived in Congo, I was acutely aware of my Americanness. But now that I was back in the United States, I always felt just a little foreign, as though I carried that sensation home with me.

Sometimes, standing in a crowded subway car, I would study the faces of the other passengers, heads tilted back. I'd think of my first neighbors in Goma, how Mama Kavira had barely known me but still called out to me in that sing-song voice, "Mzungu, what did you buy for me at the market today?" She'd asked that same question day after day, never giving up.

Her question had been a joke, and I had gritted my teeth at the time. Only now, as I write this book, do I realize that Mama Kavira's question was also gift, an invitation to community.

In New York, I sat there on those subway cars, watching passengers refuse to make eye contact, and it bothered me for the first time. Sometimes, when I found myself nearly drowning in the anonymity, I imagined implementing Mama Kavira's strategy on the subway in New York City. I pictured catching the eye of a passenger across the way and gesturing to the bags she was carrying.

"What did you buy for me at the market today?" I could hear myself call out in a sing-song voice.

My fellow passenger would probably look away.

But maybe not. New Yorkers often surprised me. That passenger might have smiled at my ridiculous question. It might have carried her back to some other place or some other time. She might have laughed and tipped the bag to reveal high-heel shoes in her plastic shopping bag, and that she was headed home from a day at the office. Or maybe, if I was lucky, she might even have taken my invitation and played it back to me, offering me some loaf of bread hidden within her plastic bag.

Sitting on that subway car, I remained silent just like everyone else. I trained my eyes on the ceiling. But I wished I could will myself into Mama Kavira's boldness—the type of boldness that comes only from the realization that we, all of us, have nothing left to lose.

CHAPTER FORTY-NINE

A Mother's Love

I found a job teaching ESOL (English to Speakers of Other Languages) to adults in my neighborhood. The students amazed me, coming to class after long days spent cleaning other people's houses, bussing tables at restaurants or folding clothes in a laundromat. Many of my students had come to the United States as undocumented immigrants. I asked them to write stories of their lives, and they wrote of entire lives they had left behind. They wrote of farms that had disappeared, of rural livelihoods that had become impossible, and of the fear and violence that had overtaken their countries. Their stories reminded me of the villages of Congo, achingly beautiful and forever lost.

After class, one student named Cristina leaned toward me, her brown hair falling in her face. She told me in whispered tones of the son she had left in her country. "See, this is my son," she said, pointing at a picture on her phone. "This is from his second birthday, right before I left." She paused and looked proud for a moment. Then her face crumpled. "He's five now," she confessed.

Cristina told me how she called her son every day. She told me that she sent all her money home to her family. "He'll have a chance to go to school this way," she said. Then she continued,

"When I left, I promised I would see him again soon. I am not sure he remembers that anymore."

I stared at Cristina. "I am so sorry," I said, imagining her disembodied voice floating through the phone lines to her son day after day.

Another student whispered her story to me in reverse. Rosa was a plump, middle-age woman with grandchildren of her own living nearby. But she talked of her mother back in Mexico with a yearning that cut across years.

"How long has it been since you saw your mother?" I asked.

"Thirty-one years." That answer sat right on the tip of her tongue, as though she counted that number every day of her life. I did the math, trying to calculate how old Rosa's mother might be, how many years the mother and daughter might have before the chance to see each other in this lifetime forever slipped away. Mothers separated from sons. Daughters separated from mothers. I tried to imagine how any of it made sense.

CHAPTER FIFTY

Fierce

Walking home from my ESOL class one day, I passed a taco truck grilling onions and a woman selling tamales out of a cart. Waves of nausea rolled over me at the scent of the food, and I stumbled up the hill toward home. By the time I reached my house, my body had been drained of all energy. I could do nothing more than sprawl out on the bed before me. The next morning, I awoke feeling better and poured myself a cup of coffee. But as I raised the cup to my lips, it smelled unbearably bitter and I dumped it into the sink. Nothing about the world seemed to stay in its place that day, as though I was living in someone else's body. Finally, I realized I was pregnant.

"Felicidades!" the students in my ESOL class shouted.

"Felicitations!" Argentine and Mapendo exclaimed over the phone. "I was starting to worry that you wouldn't have any children!" Argentine added with a laugh, giving voice to a thought that many of my ESOL students probably shared.

A few months later, a doctor looked at my chart and told me that I was a carrier for a genetic mutation for cystic fibrosis. "Don't worry, it's very unlikely that your husband will also have a mutation. It isn't a problem unless you are both carriers, and even then, it is only a one in four chance that your baby will inherit both mutations," the doctor said.

The doctor went on and on with statistics and percentages. But it didn't matter what else the doctor said that day.

In that moment, I knew everything. I knew that my husband would carry the genetic mutation. And I knew that six months later my daughter would be diagnosed with cystic fibrosis. I googled cystic fibrosis and the words *pediatric mortality* appeared on the screen. The bottom fell out of my world.

I understood, then, the fierce desperation born in every mother whose child faces a future that suddenly narrows. I understood why Cristina had handed over her two-year-old son, breaking her own heart, just to scrub floors in someone else's country, just to earn enough money to send her son to school, just for a chance to try and pry her son's future from the hands of fate.

I thought of Mapendo's mother scrambling for two tickets to Goma, with nothing to sell but a tree that was not yet grown. I thought of Argentine's mother carrying Argentine into the forests and hiding her in a hole. "The bullets can't reach you here," she had promised. She must have turned around and whispered a prayer.

As the doctor talked, it became overwhelmingly clear to me that there was nothing I could do. I could only wait. My daughter's fate lay somewhere outside of myself. And yet, as I sat there in the office with genetic counselors who talked about life like a roulette wheel, I knew two things for certain.

I knew that I would give anything for my child to be okay.

And I knew that every mother in the world feels exactly the same.

CHAPTER FIFTY-ONE

Born

December 2011

Six months later, my little girl was born with both genetic mutations for cystic fibrosis. "She is fine for now," the specialist told us. "Bring her back every six months for tests."

Holding my daughter to my chest, her warm body snuggled next to mine, I tamped down the fears in the back of my head. "Fine for now," was enough. It had to be.

CHAPTER FIFTY-TWO

A Home

Every time I talked to Mapendo on the phone, she talked about her mother. Her mother was living in an IDP (Internally Displaced People) camp at the edge of Goma. Quietly, for over a year, Mapendo had saved up her sewing money, until one day she had enough money to build her mother a house on a small piece of land in Sake. She sent me a list of the supplies she was buying. Wood. Nails. Tin for the roof. Cement for the floor. Finally, Mapendo called and told me. "The house is finished. I built my mother a house."

Mapendo's mother moved out of the refugee camp. I thought of all the years she had sought shelter in Sake, in the shadow of someone else's living room. How amazing that she would finally have her own home. How amazing that her youngest daughter had built it. I could feel Mapendo's pride every time that we talked.

CHAPTER FIFTY-THREE

Walking in the Dark

A few months later, Mapendo called again in that same steady voice. "Dada, I am going to get married." Joseph, Mapendo's fiancé, was a man she had met through the sitball team. He had polio as a child, but he had fought to go to school and had managed to finish secondary school as well as several years at university.

A few months after her marriage, Mapendo called again to say that she was pregnant, and this time her voice wobbled just a little with the enormity of all that lay before her.

For months, Mapendo nervously counted down toward her due date. The doctors had told her to wait for her water to break and then go to the hospital.

By that time, many of Mapendo's friends from the Centre pour Handicapés had given birth. All of them had given birth via C-Section. Mapendo looked down at her growing belly, and then at her leg in the metal brace and her hip jutting outward.

Both Riziki and Solange had also gotten married around the same time as Mapendo. Two months before Mapendo's due date, Solange gave birth to a little girl. The baby was born healthy, but the c-section had been complicated, and Solange's recovery was difficult. Mapendo grew more and more nervous.

For Mapendo, contractions started during the day. They were mild, and she didn't think it was time to go to the hospital yet, so she waited at home for her water to break. The sun rose high in the sky, then started to set. Joseph looked at the sun fading into the horizon and said, "If you want to go to the hospital, we should go now before it gets dark."

Mapendo declined. With her steady determination, she was still waiting for her water to break. It was midnight when she thought she felt her water break. She looked down to discover blood instead. The doctor had told her that if she saw blood, she needed to come to the hospital right away. It was midnight in Goma. Mapendo looked from the blood to the darkness outside. She held her hand to her belly, then turned to her husband. "I will walk to the hospital. You stay here," she said to Joseph. Then she turned to her sixteen-year-old niece, Kahindo, who was staying with them at the time. "Kahindo can accompany me. If we go by ourselves, no one will think that we are a threat. They will see I am a disabled woman. I am pregnant. And Kahindo is just a girl. Maybe they will have mercy." Mapendo knew that a man walking in Goma in the middle of the night would be seen as a threat. It would only invite an attack. She begged Joseph to stay behind and then walked out the door and into the darkness with only Kahindo at her side.

The streets were deserted. Mapendo walked slowly down the road, leaning on her crutches, favoring her good leg. The weight of her belly, large with child, was almost unbearable. Her arms and her wrists ached from the crutches. The pace was painfully slow. But she thought of her baby and refused to turn back. She could only walk a little way before the next contraction doubled her over in pain. She stopped, sat on a rock by the side of the road, and breathed into the darkness. Then she continued forward. Mapendo and Kahindo walked this way for nearly four hours. They never saw anyone. Just as the first glow of morning light was starting to lighten the sky, they arrived at the hospital. Jonathan was born via c-section later that day.

CHAPTER FIFTY-FOUR

At Least This

"How is Mapendo?" I asked Argentine over the phone. She assured me that the Mapendo and the baby were doing well. "And what about you? How are you?" I asked. I worried that Argentine, underneath her enthusiasm, might feel left behind with so many babies arriving.

"Let me tell you something," Argentine whispered across the phone lines one day. "Wait, let me go outside where no one can hear."

In a voice that might have been excited or scared, ashamed or proud, Argentine told me she was three months pregnant. "We haven't gotten married yet." Her voice trailed off into the web of financial obligations and family expectations that young men in Congo often find difficult to navigate.

"It will be fine!" I said. "Congratulations!"

She let out a sigh of relief.

I thought of my friends often as I woke in the night to breastfeed my little girl, hushing her back to sleep. A world away, I knew that Mapendo and Solange were doing the same with their babies. I opened a SHONA box and found a tiny African dress Mapendo had sewn for my little girl. I sent back stuffed animals and cozy blankets. We traded baby stories.

Riziki's little boy, Daniel, was born a few months after Mapendo's son. He weighed one and a half kilograms when he was born. That would be under three and a half pounds. I stared at my phone looking at the pictures of tiny baby Daniel in an incubator. How could a life so fragile survive in Goma? My own daughter had been born weighing nine pounds (four kilograms). I felt the weight of her in my arms, then eight months old, and imagined Riziki's feather-weight son. Riziki stayed in the hospital for two months with her son, hardly daring to breathe. But somehow, he grew, and finally mother and son were released from the hospital.

In the space of nine months, Mapendo, Riziki, Solange, and I had all given birth, and Argentine was pregnant. There was joy in all of the births, but there was also the shadow of fear. It felt like we were holding something that might one day crack. One day, late in the afternoon, my phone rang, and a Congolese number flashed on the screen. I looked nervously at the incoming call, knowing it was the middle of the night in Goma.

"Baby Jonathan is sick," Mapendo said when I answered the phone. "His body's so hot." I pictured Mapendo trapped in her house in Goma, holding her son's hot body as he went limp. Malaria often spiked in the night.

"Put him in cold water to lower his temperature," I said. "Will he drink something?"

Clearly there was nothing I could do from New York. And I had no expertise anyway.

But still Mapendo, Solange, and Riziki would often call me when their babies were sick in the night. Sometimes a mother with a sick baby just wants to know that there is a voice on the other end of the line.

Eventually, the fever broke. "Au moins hiyi," Mapendo said. "At least this." The words were a mix of Swahili and French, but they made perfect sense in my soul. Every time I carried my daughter back for tests at the specialists, the doctor would say "For now, she is okay." And I would wrap her up tightly and think, *Au moins hiyi. At least this.*

CHAPTER FIFTY-FIVE

By Boat or by Kinga

November 2012

One day in November, Mapendo called me. "Vita inaanza," she said. "The war is starting."

"What do you want to do?" I asked carefully, better accustomed now to listen for the tension between Mapendo's steady words.

"We have to go," she said. "They're saying that the rebels will be here soon." My mind flashed to those days a few years earlier when we'd fled to Rwanda. I thought of the explosions and gunfire we listened to at night and the way Goma had spiraled into chaos.

"The border to Rwanda is already closed," Mapendo continued. "We want to take a boat across the lake to Bukavu."

"Yes! Go now! Before it is too late," I said.

Joseph rushed to the port to buy tickets for a boat leaving for the city of Bukavu that afternoon. Tickets in hand, he returned to the house. "It is going to be fine," he said to Mapendo, as she packed a bag for baby Jonathan. Mapendo had grown up fleeing from Kimoka to Sake, sleeping in the forests, fleeing from armed men. But this was different. This time she was carrying her son on her back.

Mapendo and Argentine called Riziki and Solange. "We have tickets to Bukavu," Mapendo said. Riziki and Solange's husbands were not home. Decisions had to be made fast. Riziki and Solange decided to join Argentine and Mapendo.

Joseph talked to a minibus driver who agreed to carry the whole group to the port. He counted them all. Joseph, Mapendo and baby Jonathan, along with Mapendo's two young nieces, Neema and Ziada. That was five. Argentine had her little sister, Aline, and her own fiancé. That was three more. Solange had her daughter on her back, and a little girl named Esther. That was three more. Riziki had her tiny son Daniel and her younger sister, Zawa.

Fourteen people climbed onto the minibus that day and started toward the port. Goma had that expectant air, as though a storm was about to arrive. Doors to shops were shutting. Motorcycle taxis were whizzing by.

Then, suddenly, just as they passed through Birere, the world lit up in chaos. Masses of government soldiers poured through the streets as they fled out of town. There was gunfire, honking, and shouting. Cars and trucks with soldiers on top raced directly towards them. Dust swirled in the air. Crowds choked the street. Pickup trucks loaded with machine guns on back raced down the road. Everything was headed straight towards their minibus with its fourteen passengers inside.

The minibus was trapped in the crowd. *We're too late,* Mapendo thought, clutching baby Jonathan to her chest. *The war has started.*

In the front seat, Argentine and Joseph were begging the driver not to abandon the vehicle. "You can't leave us here," they wailed. The possibility of arriving at the port had long ago disappeared. "At least take us back to the place where we started," they begged.

The driver relented, miraculously wheeling the minibus into a three-point turn in the midst of the crowd. He steered the minibus down the street towards the place where they had started. When they reached the gas station near Mapendo's house, gunfire was coming from everywhere.

"Shuka! Shuka!" the driver shouted. "Get down! Get down!" They crawled out of the minibus, lying on the ground, taking cover by a stairwell.

Mapendo grabbed Jonathan tighter. "Shhhhhhh," she whispered into his ear. Out of the corner of her eye, she saw tanks rolling by in the street. There were soldiers shooting and shooting without any sense. Mapendo squeezed her eyes shut.

By the time there was a break in the gunfire, it was nearly dark. There was nowhere to go but back home again. The group fled back down the street toward Mapendo and Joseph's house.

When they arrived at Mapendo's house that night, the air was still electric with the sounds of gunfire and mortars. They piled mattresses on the floor and hid underneath them. Mapendo called me that night and spoke in a muffled voice. I picked up the phone hoping to hear that they had made it safely to Bukavu. Instead, I heard the crackle of gunfire in the background. It was a terrible sound.

"Utuombee."—"Pray for us," Mapendo begged, her voice filled with too much air. Just before she clicked off the phone, I could hear the other women in the background hushing their babies, the edges of their voices ragged with fear.

That night the shooting went on and on. It was so loud that their brains became numb.

Finally, the morning came. The air had shifted in the night. Government soldiers had disappeared, and rebel soldiers had taken control of the neighborhood. "You can't stay here," rebel soldiers were shouting outside the windows. "Go find somewhere safer." The rebels were clearing out the neighborhood in anticipation of further fighting.

Outside there were no buses. No motorcycle taxis. Where could they go?

Still thinking of their original boat plan, they decided to head toward the lake. This time they knew they wouldn't make it to the main port. Instead, they hoped to find a small boat nearby at Kituku.

Argentine had a kinga, and she climbed on that. Her fiancé, who was not disabled, offered to push her along. The other women began to walk on crutches. The little girls held hands. Mapendo tied her son to her back. She could barely walk. But still, she clung to her son, refusing to let anyone else carry him. Mapendo knew that in war, plans fall apart. Friends and family are lost and separated. Children are torn from mothers. Mapendo refused to give her child to anyone.

When the group reached Kituku, they realized there was no way they would find a boat. Gunfire erupted again. For a while, they took shelter in a half-built house by the side of the road. The little girls covered their ears. The babies cried. Then they headed out again.

At some point, the group broke apart.

Argentine's fiancé was pushing Argentine in her kinga, making a steady pace. Argentine could think of nothing but her baby still waiting to be born. Each time Argentine heard gunfire, pain would shoot through her belly. She was determined to leave Goma.

"Don't leave me behind!" Solange begged Argentine. "Let me ride on the back of your kinga."

Argentine agreed. Solange handed her baby to Argentine. Argentine tied Solange's six-month-old baby onto her chest with an African cloth. The weight of Solange's baby pushed heavy against Argentine's belly, now five months pregnant, and for a moment Argentine thought she wouldn't be able to breathe.

Solange climbed on the back of the kinga. Argentine looked at her sister, Aline, eight years old, standing to the side of the kinga, already disappearing into the crowded road. She grabbed Aline's thin wrist sharply and tied a brightly colored kitenge cloth around it. Argentine tied the other end of the kitenge to the kinga. "Stay by my side," she said. Then Argentine turned to little Esther, Solange's relative, only seven years old. Argentine tied another kitenge cloth to Esther's wrist, and then attached that to the other side of the kinga. Flanked by little girls on both sides, with Solange riding on back, a baby tied to her chest, and another one kicking inside, Argentine sat in her kinga and faced straight down the road. She pushed her hand pedals, but the metal tricycle didn't move. Then, from behind, Argentine's fiancé pushed the kinga forward, and they began to roll.

The roads were full of panicked people carrying mattresses and children and bundles on their heads. Tanks rolled by. Pickup trucks with artillery flew past. Soldiers rushed by on motorcycles. Other soldiers walked along the road, sometimes they came up behind Argentine's kinga and began pushing it along. "Let me help you, sister," they said as they all fled together.

A truck carrying injured government soldiers stopped alongside Argentine. "Sister, where are you going? Get in the truck with us," the soldiers offered Argentine. For a moment, Argentine pictured riding with the soldiers, but suspicion crept up her spine. She shook her head, and before she could open her mouth, the truck had raced away.

All day, Argentine pedaled, and her fiancé pushed. The little girls walked by the side, and their legs began to swell with exhaustion. They had no water. No food. The bullets were flying so close that sometimes Argentine thought she had been hit.

When they drew near to the town of Sake, Argentine saw mai-mai soldiers walking the other direction, heading toward Goma. Instead of regular clothes, they were dressed for war in skirts fashioned out of leaves, with belts of bullets hanging off their bare chests and weapons in their hands. The mai-mai are a form of local militia in Congo, young men who were often recruited to fight with the promise of a traditional medicine so powerful it would make them fearless and bulletproof. Argentine pedaled through Sake half-hiding from the wild look in the eyes of the mai-mai soldiers, until suddenly she saw a face that she recognized. *That is Chrétien,* Argentine thought to herself in surprise, remembering a boy she had originally met at the Centre pour Handicapés many years earlier. He had been at the Center caring for a disabled relative.

The shadow of Chrétien's face grew closer and closer until it was undeniable. Argentine glanced at the weapon in his hands, the bare chest, and the skirt fashioned from leaves. But she saw only the little boy she had known years ago. For just a moment, Chrétien raised his hand in greeting, then he let it fall back down.

Sometime after dark, Argentine and Solange arrived in a village fifteen kilometers (nine miles) from Minova. Solange had relatives there. They arrived at the door thinking there would be food to eat, but Solange's relatives were so poor they had nothing to give. Argentine and her group collapsed on the dirt floor anyway.

Argentine took her cell phone out. All day she had left it hidden under her shirt, pressed against her skin. She was afraid that soldiers would steal it, or simply that the battery would run out. Argentine switched the cell phone on, anxiously looking at the icon in the corner to see how many bars of power remained. Then she called me.

"Dada, we will make it to Minova tomorrow," Argentine said.

"Wait, where is Minova?" I asked, trying to calculate whether I could send money via Western Union to Minova. I knew they would run out of cash soon. I pulled up a map of the region and studied the route, wishing my husband were nearby. My husband would know where Minova was. But my husband was traveling for work and I was in my apartment in Brooklyn alone with my eleven-month-old daughter. I prayed my friends' phones would keep working.

"Dada, there are soldiers everywhere. I don't think any banks will be open in Minova," Argentine said.

"Then don't stop. Just keep going," I replied.

I stared at the map: Goma to Sake, then Sake to Minova. My friends were circling around Lake Kivu, from one town to another. Their only option was to keep going forward, but they were still a long way from the only major city I could see, the one on the other end of the lake, 150 km away. They had to make it all the way to Bukavu, the same city they had originally tried to reach by boat.

"Where are Mapendo and Riziki?" I asked, picturing Mapendo with baby Jonathan on her back and Riziki with her tiny son Daniel.

"I don't know," Argentine replied as she clicked off the phone.

CHAPTER FIFTY-SIX

Minova

The next day Argentine, her fiancé and Solange returned to the road. The little girls' legs were swollen from the previous day of walking, and they could no longer carry themselves. They clung to the edge of the kinga while Argentine's fiancé pushed. As they made their way forward, hushed stories floated through the air.

"The soldiers stole all of our goats last night," someone whispered. "They pillaged that shop."

"The girl in that house was raped," someone else said.

"Our neighbor was killed," another reported.

Just as they neared Minova, a friend from Goma called Argentine. The woman on the other end of the line said, "Whatever you do, don't stay in Minova!" But it was too late, they were almost there, and besides, the only way out was through.

Argentine's phone rang again. This time it was Mapendo.

"Mapendo, where are you?" Argentine demanded.

"Goma," Mapendo answered. Her voice trembled.

"You're still in Goma? A lot of people have already died there!" Argentine shouted into the phone.

"'I know. I'm trying to leave," Mapendo said. "We'll meet in Minova."

CHAPTER FIFTY-SEVEN

By Motorcycle

Back in her home in Goma, Mapendo tucked her phone close to her skin. This time she was determined to make it to Minova.

Mapendo was scared and frustrated. She couldn't believe she was still stuck in Goma, two days after she had first tried to leave. The previous day, Mapendo, Joseph, and Riziki had been hiding in a half-built house when they heard the rebels on the radio announcing that they had taken control of Goma. "Go back to your houses. Go back to life as normal," the rebels were saying.

"Tusiende. Fujo imeisha," Joseph had said. "Let's not leave. The fighting is finished." Joseph kept his voice low and confident, knowing how fear can push a person into the mouth of disaster.

They went back to their house that night. Mapendo fought the fear in her chest. Bullet holes riddled their walls. They locked the door that night, but there was no sleeping as they listened to the sounds of mortars and shooting.

When the morning arrived, Mapendo straightened up and began to make her plans. She turned to Joseph. "I will not stay here another night. I am going to look for a motorcycle taxi. If I find one, I am going to take it to Minova." Mapendo put Jonathan on her back and tied a kitenge cloth over top. She grabbed her crutches and ducked out the door.

With Jonathan on her back and her crutches on her arms, Mapendo couldn't carry anything. The bag of baby things that she had so carefully packed a couple days before had long since disappeared, forgotten in the minibus days earlier. She didn't have a diaper, blanket or an extra set of clothes for the baby. She had only thirty dollars, her cell phone and her baby.

Mapendo found a motorcycle taxi at the corner. "How much to Minova?" she asked the young motard.

"Give me twenty dollars" he said. Mapendo agreed and lifted herself onto the motorcycle, sitting sidesaddle and leaning forward to balance the weight of Jonathan on her back. She traveled the same road as Argentine but a day later. When gunfire got close, the motard would stop the motorcycle and they would dive to the ground. In the pause that followed the gunfire, they climbed back on the motorcycle and continued forward.

On the sides of the road, Mapendo could see homes that had been pillaged, doors standing open. She passed by people who had been beaten, or hit by bullets, their bodies laid out on the sides of the road. Mapendo held on to the back of the motorcycle and tried to look away. After a while it all became a blur.

When they reached the town of Sake, Mapendo looked at the streets of her childhood, now strangely empty. Sake was a ghost town with most of the people having fled or locked themselves behind their doors.

Just as they passed through Sake, the driver stopped. "I'm sorry, but I can't take you any further," the motard told Mapendo. "It isn't safe for me anymore. The soldiers will steal this motorcycle. I have to turn back."

Mapendo struggled to breathe. “Nihurumie,” she begged. “Have mercy on me.” Mapendo tried to imagine what she would do if the motorcycle left her in this abandoned town.

“I have ten dollars more. I will give you that if you get me to Minova,” Mapendo said, promising away all of her money. The driver studied Mapendo’s face, and then he nodded in agreement. The motorcycle continued down the road.

Just as the motard had feared, a soldier wielding a gun soon forced them to stop. “Shuka!” “Get down!” the soldier ordered Mapendo. He began to climb on the motorcycle in Mapendo’s place, intending to leave her standing there in the road. Other soldiers nearby began to shout. “Don’t you have any shame?” How can you steal a motorcycle from a disabled woman with a baby?” The soldier relented, motioning for Mapendo to slide forward on the motorcycle, then climbing on behind her, his gun clicking against the metal frame of the motorcycle.

They rode that way, with Mapendo and baby Jonathan sandwiched between the soldier and the motard. A few minutes later, a woman waved wildly at Mapendo, motioning for them to stop. Mapendo recognized the woman’s face from Sake.

“Mama wako alisha choka mu njia. Iko nyuma,” the woman said. “Your mother got exhausted along the way. She’s back behind us.”

What can I do? Mapendo thought. She couldn’t return for her mother. She had to keep going with her baby.

They passed through a town where a government commander was attempting to reorganize his troops. The commander came rushing toward the motorcycle, and Mapendo’s heart beat fast.

Then in a flash, the commander pulled the soldier down from the motorcycle. “Unafanya nini?” he demanded angrily. “What are you doing? Don't you have any shame?" the commander shouted at the soldier.

Mapendo, Baby Jonathan, and the motard sped away, leaving the soldier to face his fate. Eventually they made it to Minova. Mapendo thanked her driver.

When she arrived in Minova, Mapendo called Argentine. They arranged to meet on the outskirts of town. As she waited, Mapendo cast her eyes around Minova. There were soldiers everywhere. And something was different here. The soldiers were no longer running. They were drinking beer and smoking cigarettes and sitting on white plastic chairs outside small shops that they had forced open.

Mapendo's back was exhausted from carrying Jonathan. She leaned on her crutches and cast her gaze away from the soldiers. *I hope Argentine arrives soon*, she thought nervously. Finally, Argentine arrived, along with Solange. "We have to get out of here," Mapendo whispered. "There are no people here, just soldiers."*

As the group organized, Riziki miraculously appeared on a motorcycle that her husband was driving, with baby Daniel tied to her back. Mapendo squinted her eyes and saw that her nieces, Neema and Ziada were riding along with Riziki. But Joseph was nowhere to be found. Where is my husband? Mapendo asked herself.

---

* Minova was the site of mass atrocities during this time period. https://www.hrw.org/report/2015/10/01/justice-trial/lessons-minova-rape-case-democratic-republic-congo

CHAPTER FIFTY-EIGHT

The Swamp and the Lake

Joseph was far behind. When Mapendo left Goma, Joseph had stayed behind with Neema, Ziada, Riziki, Baby Daniel, and Riziki's sister, Zawa. Riziki sent Zawa back to her house to get supplies for the baby, but then a few minutes later, Riziki's husband appeared with a motorcycle. "Get on quickly! I don't have much time," her husband called out. Riziki and Joseph looked at each other. Zawa had not yet returned and they couldn't all fit on the back of one motorcycle. Their heads spun from trying to figure out the next right decision. Nothing was making sense. *Who should stay and who should go? Which would be safer?* These were choices no one should have to make.

"I'll stay behind." Joseph said. Riziki climbed on the motorcycle along with Neema and Ziada, and they disappeared into the chaos of the crowded road.

A little while later, Zawa returned carrying a bundle of clothing and diapers, but Riziki and the baby were gone. Only Joseph remained in the house.

Joseph looked out from the doorway of the house and sighed. He knew the road out of town would be difficult and dangerous, full of soldiers in a chaotic retreat. His metal leg brace was cracked, and he knew he could barely walk with it, even with his forearm crutch. Still, Mapendo and baby Jonathan had disappeared down the road. They were his blood, and he was determined to follow them.

He and Zawa locked the door to their house and left, with Zawa carrying the bundle of baby things on her head, and Joseph leaning heavily on his crutch, his broken leg brace cutting a wound into his thigh. By the time they reached the main road, there were no empty motorcycle taxis. Every taxi already had three passengers crammed behind the driver.

Surprisingly, they found a bus headed to Sake. *Really? Will this bus take us to Sake?* Joseph wondered, knowing that at the edge of Sake was a roadblock full of government soldiers. *That will be the frontlines in this fight,* Joseph thought to himself. Then he thought of Mapendo and Jonathan somewhere up ahead, and he climbed on the bus.

The bus pushed down the road. Before they reached Sake, the bus stopped, and everyone climbed out. The roadblock where Joseph had expected to see soldiers was strangely empty. Everything in Sake was empty.

Joseph walked slowly, the wound cutting deeper into his leg, until he could barely move. Up ahead he saw a young man standing by the road with his motorcycle. Joseph's heart jumped, and he rushed toward the motard.

"I'll give you twenty dollars to take us to Minova," Joseph said, gesturing to himself and Zawa. The motard's face lit up.

"Tuende. Tuende mbiyo," he said. "Let's go. Let's go quickly."

But the motorcycle had no gas. The motard ran to his boss's house to ask for gas to fill up the motorcycle. The boss looked at the chaos in the street and then back again at the motard.

"You want to take my motorcycle out there right now?" he asked the motard. "That is a sure way to lose my motorcycle.

The soldiers will grab it in an instant." He shut the door, refusing to let the motorcycle out of his sight.

Joseph and Zawa were still standing there trying to figure out what to do when they heard gunfire. They looked up to see the figure of a soldier stumbling down the road. He was drunk, waving his gun in the air and firing wildly. They leapt out of the way.

After the soldier had gone, Joseph and Zawa continued walking down the road out of Sake. Soon they reached a place in the road where the deep waters of the lake stretched on one side of the road, and a muddy swamp had formed on the opposite side. There would be nowhere to hide on this stretch of the road. *If we are attacked here, we're trapped,* Joseph thought to himself in desperation. It was the story of their lives—a road caught in the space between one danger and another.

Joseph and Zawa continued along the road with Joseph limping heavily. More soldiers passed by. "Congo yetu inaharibika sana." "Our Congo, it's very broken," the retreating soldiers said, shaking their heads and sucking their teeth as if they were merely impartial observers.

Finally, a motorcycle taxi appeared with only two passengers. Joseph flagged the motorcycle down. He climbed on the back, taking the bundle of baby things from Zawa. Sitting on the motorcycle taxi, with the bundle hanging off his back, Joseph nearly toppled every time the motorcycle made a turn. The motorcycle driver stopped ten kilometers (six miles) short of Minova. Joseph climbed off the motorcycle. As he began to walk again, he carried the bundle of baby things, and the sore on his leg rubbed painfully against his leg brace. When he neared Minova, Zawa caught up to Joseph, and the two continued on together.

When Joseph and Zawa reached Minova, they saw the town full of soldiers. Nervously, they turned on a side road toward the village where Riziki's family lived. Suddenly, they caught sight of Riziki and Zawa's brothers coming down the road toward them.

"Have you seen Riziki?" Zawa asked.

"Have you seen Mapendo?" Joseph asked.

"They've all gone on to a Nyabibwe," the boys answered. "They asked us to wait for you here."

It was getting dark, and the sky was growing heavy with clouds.

"We have to go on," Joseph said, desperate to find Mapendo and Jonathan. Nyabibwe was a small village further along the lake. Joseph and Zawa walked back toward the center of Minova to look for a motorcycle taxi to carry them to Nyabibwe. But it was growing dark. The air rippled with tension. Soldiers were everywhere, drunk and unruly. No motard wanted to take the risk of being caught on the open road, at dark, in the middle of a war.

Finally, Joseph found one motard that agreed to take them to Nyabibwe. "Sit on the motorcycle and hold your crutch high in the air, so everyone knows you are not a soldier," the motard instructed Joseph, as though a crutch might be a flag of peace.

The motorcycle raced down the road. They passed through the rural village where Joseph's family lived, and they slowed for a speedbump.

"Joseph! Joseph!" someone called out to him. Joseph turned and caught sight of an aunt standing nearby, motioning to him. But Joseph couldn't stop. "Tell Mama and Papa that I have come through here. Tell them I am okay," he called out. Then the motorcycle raced on into the darkness.

Drops of rain began to pour from the sky, and the wind whipped the rain against their faces like shards of glass. Soon their clothing was soaked, and they were shivering with cold in the darkness.

Finally, Joseph and Zawa reached Nyabibwe. It was dark. Their clothes were wet. Joseph's cell phone had no more power, and he had no idea where to find Mapendo. Thoughts spun through Joseph's head. *Where could they have gone?*

He and Zawa went to a local guest house run by a family friend. They warmed themselves by a small charcoal fire, hoping their clothing would dry. Joseph found a place to charge his phone. When his phone was charged, he called Mapendo.

Mapendo and Jonathan along with Argentine, her fiancé, Riziki, Solange, Neema, Ziada, Aline, Esther, and the babies were all together at a small house down the road. They had arrived in Nyabibwe with nowhere to go, and they had asked for shelter at someone's house. The woman, a stranger, had opened her door to all of them.

Joseph sighed, relieved to know his wife and child were safe nearby. Then he and Zawa stepped away from the warmth of the fire and walked out into the darkness, wet clothes still clinging to their bodies. Joseph was unwilling to rest until, at long last, they were together again.

CHAPTER FIFTY-NINE

The Only Place Left

From Nyabibwe, Mapendo sent me a message: "Dada, tomorrow we will take motorcycle taxis to Bukavu." I was relieved to know that my friends were all together again. But I was petrified about what would happen next. Their lives had fallen into a spiral, and it was hard to imagine a way out.

When the group reached Bukavu, they found that the city was relatively calm. They collected the money I had sent to them and rented rooms in an inexpensive guest house. For a moment, they breathed. But soon they realized that the guest house staff was looking at them suspiciously, wondering how long their money would hold out. It was clear that they couldn't stay there for long.

Bukavu is a city built on a hill. It was rainy season, and the women could barely walk in their metal leg braces on the steep hills. They slid on the mud at every step. The group looked for a house to rent in Bukavu, but the inexpensive houses were all high up on the hills, and they were afraid that they would pay the advance on a house and then Bukavu might collapse into chaos as well. Rebels were still holding control of Goma, and government forces were regrouping.

They wanted to cross the border into Rwanda, thinking it would remain more stable. Joseph crossed first and found a house to rent on the Rwandan side, paying a down payment and receiving the keys to the house. But when the rest of the group tried to cross the border, they were stopped by officials eyeing the large number of children. "Where are their birth certificates?" the officials demanded. Of course, they had no paperwork. They had left without even diapers. The official shook his head and sent them back towards Congo.

For a week, the group stayed in Bukavu, trying to negotiate a way across the border, but it started to feel futile, like the only place to go was the place they had started.

Goma was still under rebel control. Argentine and Mapendo called friends and family who had remained in Goma. "Is it safe to return?" they asked again and again. But who could know the answer to that question, especially for a group of disabled women? After a few weeks, the rebels withdrew from Goma, and government soldiers returned. Argentine and Mapendo, along with their whole group boarded a bus and returned to Goma. They retraced their entire journey around the lake. Along the way they passed by government soldiers, also returning to Goma. These were the same soldiers who had fled just a few weeks earlier—the same soldiers who had been shooting, stealing motorcycles, and raping women. The crowd was no different, only the direction had changed.

People don't always return home because it is safe. Sometimes there's just nowhere else to go.

CHAPTER SIXTY

We Are Awake

December 2012

In December of that year, twenty-one first-graders were killed at Sandy Hook Elementary School, fifteen miles from the town where I grew up.

I held my daughter tighter and tried to make sense of this unexpected violence. Sandy Hook is a section of Newtown, Connecticut—the kind of picturesque New England town where I had never imagined something like this could happen.

Across the world, my friends lived in a reality where violence was expected every day. Nobody was surprised by the horrors visited on eastern Congo. A few weeks after taking the city of Goma, the rebels withdrew, leaving the city further destabilized. At night Goma teetered on the edge of lawlessness, with armed men breaking into one home after another. Rumors multiplied that rebels would soon retake the city, starting the cycle all over again.

Mapendo called me often. "We don't sleep at night," she whispered into the phone like a confession. "We stay up all night listening for attackers outside. We do everything we can, but it is never enough. We set up our own alarm systems—piling rocks in towers on the ground near the window, ready to topple when thieves approach. We spread gravel on the ground and wait for the crunching sound of footsteps."

I pictured Mapendo and Joseph then, in their small wooden shack, with children sleeping next to them. I pictured them sitting in bed listening for the sound of footsteps on gravel. I heard their voices calling out in the darkness, "We are awake! We are awake!"

CHAPTER SIXTY-ONE

Again

When Argentine returned to her house in Goma, she found bullet holes in the walls. *What would have happened if I had been inside?* Argentine asked herself, tracing the holes with her fingertips, then clutching her growing belly, six months pregnant.

Three weeks after returning to Goma, Argentine decided that she could stay no longer. She and her fiancé packed up her sewing machine, placing it in the bottom of a large woven plastic bag, surrounding it with a few clothes. This time they fled to Burundi, taking first a boat and then a bus.

At the time, they didn't think of themselves as refugees, just people looking for a safer place to live.

At the border crossing, Argentine and her fiancé insisted that they were going to visit a friend, showing the border authorities a tattered paper with her friend's name on it.

Argentine's friend, Promesse, was a Congolese woman who Argentine had met at the Center in Goma. The two young women had received treatment for their disabilities together. And afterward, Promesse had married a man from Burundi and returned to his country to live with him. This was the only person Argentine knew in all of Burundi. She had no phone number for Promesse, just her name and the name of a town where she was now working at another center for people with disabilities.

After a very long day, Argentine and her fiancé arrived in the small town in Burundi where Promesse lived. They showed their tattered note to people, and eventually someone showed them the way to Promesse's house.

"Hodi," they called out at the door.

Promesse peered out from the doorway, then rushed to hug Argentine, ushering her inside.

Exhausted, Argentine sank down, letting go of her crutches and resting her hands on her belly.

They shared a meal that night, and Argentine felt thankful to have arrived safely.

The next morning Promesse's husband shook Argentine awake. "You have to go," he said to Argentine. "Look at you, coming to our house pregnant. You are refugees. You have to go."

Argentine, exhausted from the travel, begged to stay just a few more days to build up her strength.

"You have to go now," Promesse's husband said in a firm voice. He told her to go to a refugee processing center in the capital. Argentine and her fiancé boarded a bus for the long ride back to Bujumbura, the capital of Burundi. Late into the night, they arrived at the refugee processing center. They banged on the big metal gates, and the guards opened them.

When they arrived, Argentine walked into an enormous room, full of refugees lying shoulder to shoulder. She thought she might collapse. But then an old woman saw her. "Karibu," the woman called out in Swahili. "Welcome." The old woman pointed to a place for Argentine to sit. Then she handed her a cup of tea.

"Asante," Argentine murmured. "Thank you." She drank the tea, warm and sweet.

A few days later, Mapendo decided to leave Goma as well and join Argentine in Burundi. She arrived at the refugee processing center with Joseph, Jonathan, and Ziada. It was Christmas Eve when they arrived, and their lives as refugees were about to begin.

CHAPTER SIXTY-TWO

The Camps

When Argentine, Mapendo and their families arrived in that refugee processing center in the capital city of Bujumbura, they didn't know what to expect. They found a place to sleep and did the best they could to survive. After a few weeks, they were sent to a rural camp, a day's bus ride from the capital. They were assigned small huts with plastic sheeting for the roofs and walls built from clay. Argentine and Mapendo sat on dirt floors and took out their sewing machines, placing them on small stools on the ground. They started to sew. Sometimes at night it was cold, but they sat around the fire and warmed themselves. They were thankful just to be safe. *I hope everyone is okay in Goma,* Mapendo thought to herself, remembering all the family she had left behind. *I wish I could have brought my mother with me.*

CHAPTER SIXTY-THREE

Back and Forth

Three months into her stay at the refugee camp, Mapendo's phone rang with calls from Goma. Her mother was sick in the hospital. Her mother had lost consciousness. Her mother might not make it through the week.

Mapendo faced an impossible choice—the same choice faced by many families split over borders. She could remain in the refugee camp, where she felt relatively safe, or she could take the risk of returning to Goma to see her mother who she loved dearly.

There is a myth about refugees. It is the idea that they have made one distinct journey, with a clear beginning and a clear ending. The reality for Mapendo, Argentine, and countless others is that they have made many journeys, running in circles again and again, unsure where they were headed but always hoping one day to arrive back home—hoping that one day home would be safe.

Mapendo decided to board a bus with her son and her niece, Ziada. She would visit her mother and see how conditions looked. Meanwhile, Joseph would remain in the refugee camp, keeping their place in the camp. If they both left together, they would lose their refugee status, so they decided on this course, keeping one foot planted in the refugee camp and another leading them home.

When she arrived in Goma, Mapendo rushed to the hospital to visit her mother. She paid her mother's hospital bill and bought her medicine. Mapendo's mother grabbed her hand. "Thank you for coming," she said, "but don't stay in Goma too long."

Mapendo called me from Goma. "Send some money for fabric," she told me. "I will buy more cloth before I go," she said. The fabric in Goma was cheaper. And it was familiar.

I sent Mapendo the money.

That night, Mapendo heard thieves at her door and her window. She was staying in a tiny wooden house by herself with Neema, Ziada and baby Jonathan. Terror rushed through her body.

"We are awake. We are awake," Mapendo called out into the night. Then silence.

Mapendo thought of the money tucked away in her things. Who could have known that she had that money? Her mind darkened with suspicions. *Did the thieves see me receiving the money at the bank? Did they follow me home? Is it my neighbors? Is it someone I know?*

The next morning Mapendo's phone rang with a call from Solange. Thieves had come to Solange's house in the night. They had broken down the door. They waved guns and demanded money. Solange had given them what she had, but it wasn't much.

"We'll be back again soon. Next time you better have more money," the attackers had threatened.

We'll be back soon. The words haunted Mapendo and Solange. They called me and explained what had happened. I thought of the money I had sent. Every time I sent money, I held my breath. Money bought food and medicine. It built houses. It was impossible to live without. But it was also dangerous. Like Joseph walking between the swamp and the lake, my friends were forever stuck between threats on both sides—poverty on one side and violence on the other.

"Whatever you do, don't go home tonight," I said to Mapendo.

Mapendo gathered Riziki and Solange, and they left their homes. They slept in a small guest house that night. They never bought the cloth they had been planning to purchase. Instead they used the money that I had sent to buy tickets for Riziki, Solange and their families to flee with Mapendo back to Burundi. When the group arrived in Burundi, Riziki and Solange were sent to the refugee transit center for several weeks of processing. Eventually, they were sent to a refugee camp in another corner of Burundi, far from the camp where Mapendo and Argentine were staying. My friends were separated again, but I hoped they would all remain safe.

CHAPTER SIXTY-FOUR

Giving Birth

February 2013

Back in the refugee camp, Argentine was making a life for herself. She was sewing, learning the local language of Kirundi, and making friends with whomever she could. She went to the clinic at the camp to ask for prenatal care.

"Don't worry. It will be fine," the staff at the camp clinic told Argentine. Her belly grew larger and larger. The baby did indeed seem to be fine.

But in New York, my mind still jumped immediately to the myriad risks facing Argentine. I remembered in detail the prenatal care I had received in New York. Lying awake at night, I cradled my own daughter in my arms and tried to imagine what it would be like to give birth in a refugee camp.

One day, I sat down at my computer in New York and googled maternal health hospitals in Burundi. I was astonished to discover a hospital way out in the country, near the refugee camp, specializing in maternal health. We sent Argentine to talk to the doctors there, offering to pay cash in advance. Refugees are not always accepted at local hospitals unless they have been transferred from the camp clinic. Thankfully, in Burundi at that time, they were welcome, as long as they could pay the bill.

But Argentine still had a month before her daughter was due. I worried about leaving her in the refugee camp eight months pregnant and fifteen kilometers (nearly ten miles) from the hospital. *What if there was an emergency? What if she needed to get to the hospital suddenly?* I remembered Mapendo and the blood in the middle of the night. I remembered her four hour walk to the hospital.

The hospital agreed to let Argentine rent a room in advance of the scheduled delivery. It was a mercy I couldn't have dreamed of. When Argentine arrived at the hospital, they sent for someone to help translate. A smiling nurse named Anastasie arrived speaking Swahili. She was Congolese. Words spilled out of Argentine, and the two became fast friends. They remain friends to this day.

Argentine's daughter, Rachelle, was born a month later, with no major complications. She had delicate features and a tiny, perfect body.

CHAPTER SIXTY-FIVE

Shipping Bags

Mapendo and Argentine never dropped a stitch. They had begun sewing again only days after they arrived in the Burundi camps. They sewed under tents of plastic sheeting, balancing their sewing machines on the dirt floors. They sewed without electricity, using charcoal irons to prepare the cloth.

I wondered how they would ever ship bags from Burundi. Argentine and Mapendo were stuck in one refugee camp while Riziki and Solange were stuck in another. Both camps were a full day's ride from the capital city. In order to ship their bags, they would have to travel to the capital with babies on their backs, and then they would have to navigate a city they did not know, in a language they did not speak.

For a while, Joseph traveled with Argentine and Mapendo into the capital, meeting up with Riziki and Solange there. Together, they were able to ship the bags and then return to the camps.

When the first box arrived at my apartment, I cut it open nervously, as though we had to prove ourselves all over again. The box still carried the faint smell of charcoal smoke. There was still an African dress for my daughter at the bottom of the box. And the bags were still sewn beautifully.

CHAPTER SIXTY-SIX

Returning

November 2013

After a year in the refugee camp, Mapendo called one day. "Dada, I am pregnant," she said slowly and deliberately.

"When is the baby due?" I asked.

"In a few months," she answered.

"Are you okay?" I continued, hearing the tension in her voice.

"I have to go home," she said. "I can't have this baby here."

Burundi was becoming increasingly tense. The maternity hospital where Argentine had given birth was no longer able to welcome refugees. The political situation in Burundi was growing increasingly unstable. "I have to go home," Mapendo said again. She began to pack her bags.

Later I asked Argentine what she planned to do.

"I cannot go home," Argentine said, with equally fierce determination.

Shortly after Rachelle was born, Argentine's sister-in-law had come to Burundi for a while. She had brought Argentine's little sister, Aline, so that the two sisters could be reunited. Aline was helping take care of the baby. A few months earlier,

Argentine's fiancé had returned to Congo. But Argentine had refused to go. She had decided to stay in the camp in Burundi. And now, even with Mapendo leaving, Argentine decided to stay alone in the camp with Aline and Baby Rachelle. Argentine remembered all too well the sounds of gunfire in Goma, and she was not convinced it was safe to return yet.

My friends were split up again. Mapendo and Joseph returned to Congo to wait for their new baby to be born. Argentine stayed in Burundi with Aline and Rachelle.

Finding herself alone in Burundi, Argentine faced the task of shipping bags on her own for the first time. Anxiously, she prepared in advance. She thought about how she would climb into and out of the bus, wearing her leg braces and handing the baby back and forth between herself and Aline. Aline, nine years old at the time, would carry the large bundle of SHONA bags. Sometimes life requires sheer determination.

After six or seven hours in the bus, Argentine, Aline, and baby Rachelle arrived in Bujumbura. They stood there, planted in place, and called out to the nearby taxis.

"I am going to EMS (an international shipping service). I will pay you whatever you ask, but please promise to take me right to the door. I cannot walk far," Argentine said to the taxi driver.

The taxi driver dropped them off directly in front of a large building. It seemed familiar, but the city was loud and overwhelming, and Argentine wasn't sure where to enter the building.

Argentine stood there leaning on her wooden crutches and looking up at the large, forbidding building. Slowly, she started to approach, bringing Aline and Rachelle with her. With every step, she could feel eyes squinting in her direction as she threw her legs forward again and again. The shopkeepers nearby stared at her hard.

"Where are you going? You don't belong in there," a shopkeeper called out. Argentine turned to look. She recognized immediately the look in the woman's eyes. This woman thought that Argentine had come to beg.

"But I am here to mail something," Argentine insisted.

"This is not the right place for you. You have to go across town to the government post office," another woman said.

"But look, I have the address here. It is for international shipping," Argentine insisted.

"Oh no, you definitely do not belong here," they replied.

Argentine turned back. She knew that the shopkeepers didn't believe she had any business in an international shipping office where the prices were high. She knew that she was at the right building. In the eyes of those shopkeepers, she just wasn't the right person.

Argentine kept her face blank and compliant. "Okay. Thank you," she said politely, forever navigating relationships as carefully as she could.

Argentine did exactly what the shopkeepers told her. She went across town to the local post office. The man at that office shook his head and pointed Argentine back to the original building.

Argentine gathered Aline and Rachelle and returned to the large imposing building. This time they made it inside, ignoring the shopkeepers' glances. They went down a long hallway and finally found the right door.

"Please help me. I am here to send a package," Argentine said to the woman who opened the door.

"Are you sure you are in the right place?" the woman asked Argentine.

"Yes, I am sending a package to the United States."

"Really?!" the woman exclaimed in amusement. "Who can you know in the United States?" she demanded, her eyes falling on Argentine's crutches. Argentine gave the woman my name and my address in New York.

"But how do you know this person? When is the last time you spoke to her?" The woman wouldn't let up.

"I spoke to her three days ago. She is my friend. We sew these bags to buy sugar and milk, so we can survive."

The woman seized Argentine's phone, checking the call record. "Let's call this mzungu that you say is your friend," the woman suggested.

"No, it is the middle of the night in New York," Argentine demurred. Finally, with nothing left to do, Argentine unknotted the cloth tied around her bag. She unzipped the woven plastic bag to reveal neatly stacked SHONA bags, each with a tag with a photo of Argentine on the front. The woman picked up one of the brightly colored bags and held it up to the light.

"Did you sew this yourself?" the woman asked, touching the perfect stitches along the edge. For the first time, the woman looked into Argentine's face.

"*You*, with your crutches, *you* sewed this?" she exclaimed again, touching the bag gently. Finally, she put the bag down. "Please rest here. You must be tired," the woman said, her tone suddenly soft and welcoming.

Then the woman disappeared into the next room. When she came back, she carried two bottles of soda and a treat for the baby. "Congratulations to you," she said to Argentine. "You are doing good work. Let me give you a drink."

CHAPTER SIXTY-SEVEN

The Next Step

In New York, I never lost that sense of wonder. I would open a box of SHONA bags sent from Argentine, Mapendo, Riziki, and Solange. I would run my hands over the stitching and picture how far these bags had come. Often the bags carried with them the dusty chalk lines the women had drawn, marking the center of their stitching.

I unpacked the boxes and stacked bags on my floor. My daughter would toddle over and topple each pile, attracted by the bright colors and fanciful designs.

Online, I retold the stories as best I could, trying to capture the amazing women whom these bags represented. I sorted, stocked, sold, and shipped the bags, late at night between the hours of my regular job.

It was a small offering, providing just enough money for my four friends to survive.

"You should get on Oprah," people in the United States said with a helpfulness that drove me crazy, as though Oprah might be just down the street at the bodega.

"You should add more women, get a big order from Macy's," others said. "You should start a non-profit and look for grants." But I had no idea how to do any of those things.

I did only what I knew I could.

I told stories. I took photos of bags and posted them on our website late at night, trusting that some individual would stumble on our website and buy that next bag.

And I prayed. I prayed that through some kind of grace, the next thing might be enough.

CHAPTER SIXTY-EIGHT

A Coup in Burundi

May 2015

For a year after Mapendo left, Argentine remained in Burundi with Aline and Baby Rachelle. But in Burundi, the political climate was growing more and more tense. The president had declared that he would run for another term. The angry opposition took to the streets, and there were rumors of a coup being planned. Burundi was falling into chaos.

This is the reality for refugees and internally displaced people in many corners of the world. The places that people flee for safety are often only one step away from chaos themselves.

Daily buses to the capital city stopped traveling. The roads were becoming unsafe. Other refugees came by Argentine's home to say goodbye.

"We are leaving now, we're going to the camps in Tanzania," they said. And always Argentine remembered the lesson she had long ago learned. *Disabled people can't be the last to flee,* she thought to herself.

Argentine knew she could never make that trip to the Tanzania camps on her own. She decided that it was time to return to Congo.

Argentine packed her bags. She loaded her sewing machine and all their possessions into that woven plastic bag and wrapped it with cloth. In another bag, she packed the SHONA bags she had sewn over the past two months. Each day she and Aline awoke at dawn, listening for news that the buses to the capital were traveling again.

Finally, her chance came. The roads were open. Aline put Rachelle on her back and she and Argentine rushed to the bus stop. They boarded the first bus to the capital.

The trip passed uneventfully. But when they arrived in the capital city and someone lifted Argentine down from the bus, she could tell something was terribly wrong.

The streets, usually loud and chaotic, had fallen strangely silent. It was the middle of the afternoon, but the shops were shuttered.

Argentine had planned to stop in Bujumbura to ship the SHONA bags to me before continuing to Congo, but now she realized that would be impossible.

With barely a pause, Argentine knew they had to leave Bujumbura immediately. They found a bus leaving for Congo and climbed on board.

When they crossed the border into Congo, Argentine breathed a sigh of relief. She didn't know what was about to break out in Burundi, but she was thankful to have left it behind her.

As their bus made its way through Congo, Argentine cast her eye toward the familiar green landscape outside.

Suddenly the bus jolted to a stop. They had stumbled into a local protest, unrelated to either the unrest in Burundi or the original conflict that they had fled in Goma. The streets were blocked by angry villagers. Suddenly the door to the bus was forced open and people rushed on board. Some men grabbed the driver, dragged him outside, and began to beat him.

A few Congolese soldiers happened to have been traveling on the bus. They slipped out the back and went to look for more soldiers for help. Meanwhile the angry crowd began to make its way through the bus, roughing people up, demanding all that they had.

"Mungu atusaidie," Argentine began to pray. "God help us."

The crowd worked its way through each seat. Finally, they got to Argentine. A man picked up one of Argentine's metal leg braces, which she had taken off and set to her side for the journey. Without those braces, Argentine could not stand. The man held Argentine's leg brace, his hand poised in the air.

And then somebody said, "Muache." "Leave her alone."

He put the leg brace back down and the crowd moved on to the next seat.

Argentine closed her eyes and prayed some more.

She heard a thump from the roof. People were on the roof of the bus, pillaging the luggage that had been tied to the top of the bus. All of Argentine's work for the past two months, plus her sewing machine, were tied up there in that ragged bundle.

Suddenly gunfire rang out. The soldiers were back with reinforcements. They fired into the air, and the crowd ran. Someone started the bus again, and it jolted down the road.

When they finally arrived at their destination, someone lifted Argentine down from the bus. Argentine glanced up. She saw her bundle still sitting proudly on the top of the roof, untouched.

CHAPTER SIXTY-NINE

In Goma

May 2015

When Argentine, Aline, and Rachelle returned to Goma, we celebrated. All four of the SHONA Congo women were back in one place. By this time, Mapendo's second son, Joachim, was nearly a year old. Rachelle was two and a half, but she was a thoughtful child, and she had grown up fast. Already, she would watch over Joachim, keeping an eye on the smaller child. I laughed at stories of Rachelle carrying miniature containers of water for Argentine and helping her around the house. "You must teach your daughter to carry water," Argentine said to me. I smiled. My daughter was still carrying a sippy cup.

Maybe next year, we will make it back to Congo, I thought to myself. My husband traveled back to the region frequently for work, but I still hadn't made it back. The challenges of traveling to Congo with a young child seemed overwhelming. *Maybe next year,* I thought.

Then I sat there, picturing a visit back to Congo. I imagined our two little girls, side by side. *Our daughters will be the best of friends,* I told myself. Rachelle could teach my daughter to carry water and greet visitors politely. My daughter would bring art supplies, and they'd paint pictures together. *Someday soon, we'll be together,* I promised myself.

CHAPTER SEVENTY

Rachelle

July 2015

And then, one day, it all fell apart. "Dada, tumepata kilio." That was the text message I received from Mapendo. It doesn't translate in English. Literally, it means, "We have gotten a mourning." It is as though mourning is something that is doled out by some force beyond our reckoning. Just like you "get sick." Or you "get lucky." The people of Goma "get mourning."

My heart plunged as I read the message further.

Argentine's daughter, Rachelle, had died.

CHAPTER SEVENTY-ONE

Stories We Cannot Tell

There are stories that I cannot tell. There are words that erase themselves from the page as soon as I write them, refusing any form of a narrative. This is one of those stories.

Rachelle's death made no sense the way it arrived unannounced. Of course, like all parents, we knew that our children were frightfully fragile. I was still bringing my daughter to the cystic fibrosis specialist every six months. When I brought my daughter to the specialist, they did throat cultures, reaching far back into her throat until she choked. They did sweat tests, wrapping her in sensors and warm clothing, then testing how salty her sweat was. But the results were always good. Until one time, when the results were not good. The doctor, who was usually cheerful and talkative, called back with a solemn note in her voice. "The results indicate high levels of concern," she said, asking us to bring our daughter back for retesting. The retest turned out fine, and the doctor later explained that my daughter's throat culture had gotten mixed up with another patient. Relief flooded over me, then a ball gathered in the pit of my stomach. I wondered who that other child was, the one to whom the bad results had belonged.

For Riziki, Solange, Mapendo, and Argentine, there had already been so many scares like that. Mapendo's sons were often sick with malaria and typhoid. So were Riziki and Solange's children. There had been so many late-night phone calls. I had held my breath and prayed so many times. We all had.

But without even thinking about it, I had always believed that we would see the disaster coming from a mile away. Maybe it was because we had stood witness to so many potential disasters rolling towards us in the night. But those disasters had always swerved out of sight at the last possible moment.

Rachelle—she didn't die in the night. She wasn't even sick in the night. One day she had a cold. The next day, she woke up. She ate breakfast that morning. Then sometime in the afternoon she got worse. Her eyes went strangely vacant. Argentine took Rachelle to a traditional medicine doctor, but that was no help. Rachelle was getting worse. Argentine and her mother climbed onto motorcycle taxis and raced Rachelle to a hospital. Rachelle died at the hospital that night.

To this day, we don't know what happened. The morning after Rachelle's death, Mapendo arrived at the hospital. She asked the doctors what happened but there was no explanation. They had tested Rachelle for malaria and typhoid, two of the most common causes of illness in Congo, but the test results showed nothing. People in Goma get sick. Sometimes they die. And often there just aren't enough medical resources to dedicate to the living, never mind investigating the cause of death for those who have departed.

Inexplicable tragedy plagues Goma. It plagues Goma in the form of armed men who break down doors in the night, leaving families to question whether they have been targeted or whether they are the victims of random violence. It plagues Goma in the form of sudden deaths without explanation. There are never enough answers and there are always cruel rumors that descend like a fog. It is hard to see out of that fog.

"Tumepata kilio," Mapendo said. "We have gotten a mourning."

Sometimes those are the only words that exist.

CHAPTER SEVENTY-TWO

Community

Through all these journeys, a community of customers and friends had collected around the SHONA Congo women. When Rachelle died, news of Argentine's loss rippled through our community. We got dozens of messages from our customers.

Please tell Argentine we are praying for her.

I, too, have lost a child.

I wake at night and pray for Argentine.

The messages went on. For years, our customers had proudly carried their SHONA bags to the supermarket. When someone commented on the bag, our customers would say, "Let me tell you about the woman who made this bag." Our customers do that still.

Argentine, Mapendo, Riziki, and Solange have returned this kind of long-distance friendship. When there was an earthquake in California, Argentine had sent a message asking if any of our SHONA friends were hurt. Often it seemed the SHONA Congo women knew of disasters in the United States before I heard of them. "Is everyone okay there?" Argentine would ask.

And now our friends in the United States, Canada, and Europe heard about this disaster which had fallen on Argentine. We mourned together.

CHAPTER SEVENTY-THREE

Alive

In Goma, friends from the Centre pour Handicapés surrounded Argentine. All those years ago, Argentine had told me about arriving in Goma for the first time, how she had trusted that stranger on the kinga simply because she was also disabled. "We are like family," Argentine had said of people with disabilities. She was right. Her family surrounded her.

Argentine was afraid to return to her own house. She faced the kind of outrageous threats that fall upon the bereaved in Goma, where families reeling from loss often find more being stolen away. Papa Ruzi, who had known Argentine since she arrived at the Center, took her in, watching over her like a father figure.

Argentine's voice sounded weak on the phone. She sounded like she was talking through the end of a very long tube, or maybe like she was talking under water. I wondered if she would ever come up for air.

She stopped eating. She couldn't sleep. She felt like there was nothing left for her in the world.

Less than a month after Rachelle died, Argentine's brother's little girl also died. The two little girls had been cousins, fast friends. I have pictures of them together, wearing party dresses and standing in front of sculptures in the middle of Goma. It was impossible to understand how they had both suddenly died.

Argentine stumbled through life. One day she climbed on her kinga and began moving her hands in a circle, pedaling toward Mapendo's house. As she pedaled, she suddenly realized that she was passing the place where they had bought Rachelle's coffin. Lost in thought, she didn't notice the minibus coming at her until it was too late.

The minibus struck Argentine's kinga. Argentine flew through the air. The bus screeched to a stop, and the driver scrambled out of the bus and fled the scene.

"Someone's been killed! Someone's been killed!" a cry rose up from the street.

The passengers climbed out of the bus, shaken and horrified. One of the passengers rushed to Argentine's body, lying there on the ground. Her head was inches from the bus's wheel.

The man began to lift Argentine's body, as a wail rose up from the crowd. Then suddenly, he shouted with excitement, "She's alive! She's alive!"

The man pulled Argentine to a sitting position, shaking her gently. "Look at you! You haven't died at all," he pronounced in astonishment.

Argentine stared up from the ground, shocked to find herself alive. Her gaze turned to the tire that had nearly crushed her head. "God kept me alive," Argentine murmured to herself. It wasn't so much a relief as simply a statement of fact—a conclusion she couldn't deny. It didn't make up for a single loss she had experienced, but it gave her a type of resolve. She began to sleep a little at night. She began to eat a little during the day.

After a few more months, she suddenly got a craving for french fries. Argentine called her brother. "Can you bring me some french fries?" His heart soared. *Argentine's finally hungry,* he thought to himself, thrilled to bring her any food that she craved. Soon after that, Argentine finally brought herself to recollect something else that she had forgotten in the recesses of her mind. It had been a while since her last period.

CHAPTER SEVENTY-FOUR

Forward

Sometimes the only way out is forward. Less than six months after Rachelle died, Argentine discovered herself pregnant again, a new life growing inside her. Argentine remembered her first pregnancy, the pain she would feel every time she heard gunfire in the air of Goma. *I must leave Goma*, she thought to herself. She called Mapendo. Mapendo was still facing her own problems, lying awake every night in a desperate vigil to keep her own sons safe from the attackers outside.

In the hushed hours of the night Argentine and Mapendo quietly put together a plan. They were tired of running, tired of gunfire, and tired of fear. They wanted the one thing that every mother wants—a safe home for their children. And just like every mother, everywhere, they would do almost anything to try and find it.

CHAPTER SEVENTY-FIVE

The Road to Bunagana

February 2016

"The road to Bunagana is dangerous," strangers told Argentine and Mapendo. "Some people make it and some people don't."

Argentine and Mapendo nodded, quietly accepting whatever the road held for them. It was their only way to Uganda, eighty-three kilometers away. After Rachelle's death, Argentine knew that she could no longer stay in Goma. She wondered where she could go. She wanted to return to her mother's house in Kitchanga, but Kitchanga was not safe. She thought about returning to Burundi, but there was an attempted coup d'état in Burundi last time she was there. Uganda was the only other option. Argentine called her mother in Kitchanga. "Come to Goma to say goodbye to us," she begged her mother. Her mother came.

"No matter where we go, I will always carry you in my heart," Argentine promised her mother.

"I will pray for you," her mother responded. They cried. And then they let go, already accustomed to a world of impossible choices.

Mapendo wanted to bring her own mother with her. She thought about it late at night, as she sat in bed and listened for thieves at her door. *My mother can't stay here*, she thought to herself. But Mapendo's mother was sick, in and out of the hospital. The journey would be long. Mapendo didn't know if her mother could make it. "Wherever I go, I will send help back to you," Mapendo promised her mother. It was the best she could do.

Mapendo and Argentine quietly prepared to leave. Argentine planned to flee with her fiancé and her younger sister Aline (age twelve). Mapendo and Joseph would bring their two sons (ages two and three) along with Mapendo's two nieces Neema and Zi-ada (ages ten and fourteen).

They would travel by bus to Bunagana. It was a gamble at best. The road to Bunagana was a terrible road. Armed men often waited by the roadside, forcing vehicles to stop, and then threatening, looting, sometimes raping or killing the passengers inside.

Still, it was the best choice that they had.

Mapendo stuffed little boy clothing into a woven plastic bag, then she brought the bag to someone else's house, so that no one would notice their preparations to leave. In Goma, anything could turn a person into a target.

The day before they were scheduled to leave, Argentine's mother knocked on Mapendo's door. "My child, I have come to say goodbye," she said. They embraced. Mapendo was happy to see Argentine's mother, but fear stuck in Mapendo's throat. Someone might have seen that goodbye they had shared. Mapendo and Joseph had cash in their hands. It was the money they needed for the next day's journey. Mapendo stood on her crutches in her small wooden home, a place that had long ago ceased to feel safe. “We cannot sleep here tonight,” Mapendo said to Joseph. “The thieves will come for us tonight.”

For their last night in Goma, Mapendo and her family abandoned their home. They slipped out the door and slept in someone else’s house. At first light, they all set out for the bus station. When they arrived there, a man piled their possessions onto the roof of a minibus, and they all climbed in.

“Mungu atusaidie,” Mapendo whispered. “God help us.”

As the minibus pulled onto the bumpy road, Mapendo began to breathe. For years Goma had felt like a trap closing in on them all. This was the answer to her prayers— a chance at safety, no matter how dangerous the road might be.

Soon the city of Goma faded into the distance, and the road emptied out. The minibus plunged into the heart of the forest. Gunfire punctuated the air.

The driver of the minibus turned to look at his passengers. “Men with guns are pillaging the mini-bus in front of us,” he whispered pointing to the road ahead, shrouded in trees. “If you have legs to carry you, get out of this bus and hide in the trees,” he said in a hurry.

One of the passengers threw the door open, and the other passengers disappeared into the trees.

Argentine’s fiancé got out of the minibus. He was able to move quickly without a disability. But Argentine, Mapendo and Joseph remained rooted in place. There was no way they could run with their crutches and leg braces. They clutched the children in their arms. “We’ll stay here together,” Mapendo whispered to the girls, unwilling to let them out of her sight. In a few minutes, the minibus had nearly emptied out and now they were the only passengers remaining.

“Don’t be afraid,” the driver whispered. Then he began to reverse the minibus down the road, inch by inch, trying to create as much distance between the vehicle and the gunfire as possible. After about ten minutes, the driver stopped the minibus again. "I'll come back," he promised. Then he too disappeared into the trees to hide.

Argentine, Mapendo, Joseph, and the children sat there in a minibus that everyone else had abandoned. Mapendo was holding her youngest son, Joachim. He started to fuss, and she gave him her breast. Mapendo nursed her child and prayed the attackers would never arrive. It was a prayer she had been saying all her life.

It felt like an hour passed, maybe two.

Then the driver of the minibus reappeared. "Tuende mbiyo," he said, as he climbed in the front seat. The minibus roared around the bend, then stopped again.

Like magic, the other passengers took shape out of the forest and hoisted themselves back into the minibus. The driver floored the gas pedal, and Mapendo's heart soared. She had no idea where they were going, but the direction was right. They were going forward.

By the time they arrived in Bunagana, it was dark. The driver helped Argentine and Mapendo down from the minibus, then he studied them carefully. "Lock the door to your room. If anyone comes to the door, don't let them in," he instructed.

The families rented rooms at a local guest house. They locked the doors, and in the darkness of those rooms they collapsed onto the beds.

CHAPTER SEVENTY-SIX

Uganda

The next day they crossed the border from Congo to Uganda. They declared themselves refugees, and they were directed to a refugee transit camp where they stayed for several weeks, thankful to be alive.

One morning, a fleet of buses arrived at the camp.

"Everyone get on the bus," someone shouted.

So, they got on the bus.

They traveled all day through barren land, far up north into the wilderness. Finally, at sunset, they arrived at another refugee camp where they were given a place to sleep that night.

This isn't so bad, Mapendo thought, her fear starting to subside.

The next morning, a truck pulled into the transit camp. Refugees fought one another to scramble on board.

Mapendo and Argentine looked at each other, unsure what everyone was fighting for.

"Where will the truck go?" Mapendo asked a Swahili-speaking woman nearby.

"These trucks go to the end of the road," the woman explained.

"Why?" Mapendo asked.

"This camp is full," the woman murmured. "I have been here for years. You are new. You must go to the end of the road."

Argentine and Mapendo sat watching the procession warily as truck after truck arrived to carry off refugees.

"Let's just wait," they decided. "Surely the officials will have mercy on us. If we just wait until everyone else is gone, they will see how disabled we are and let us stay here."

For days they waited, watching nervously as the camp emptied out. They heard stories about the place at the end of the road. They heard that it was up in the hills, where they wouldn't be able to walk with their crutches. They were told there was no shelter there and no housing to be given. Each refugee received only plastic sheeting. They would be instructed to find branches to cut down and construct a hut out of that.

Haitawezekana, Mapendo thought, shaking her head. *It will not be possible.*

Finally, there were no other new refugees left.

"Let us stay here. Look at our crutches. How can we go out there into the hills and build our own shelter?" Argentine and Mapendo said to a woman. They had heard that this woman oversaw "vulnerable populations."

But the woman shook her head. Her eyes scanned past Argentine, Mapendo, and Joseph. She scanned past the children and settled on Argentine's fiancé.

"*He* will help you build. He is not disabled," she said, pointing at Argentine's fiancé. Catching the look of despair in their eyes, the woman's voice softened a little. "Don't worry, we will come and check on you in a few days," she said.

Someone picked up their possessions and stuffed the ragged bundles onto the truck, and they climbed on board.

The truck bumped along the road, occasionally sending them flying. They held on with all that they had.

Finally, the truck reached the end of the road and spilled the passengers out into the dust. Then the truck raced off.

Mapendo lifted her eyes to the hills, overcome by the sight of rolling hills with white plastic tarps and makeshift shelters as far as the eye could see.

She looked at the barren land with only twigs and grass strewn about. Now she understood why the other refugees had fought to be first. Perhaps at one time there had been trees with branches worth cutting down, but now there was nothing.

They slept that night, at the base of the hills, gathering a few branches, bending them back to create a tiny shelter covered with plastic sheeting. Argentine, Mapendo, and the children huddled inside, lying nearly on top of each other. The men slept outside on top of their bundles so that no one would steal their only possessions.

It rained that night. The water rushed off the hills and into their tent. Then the rats came, scuttling under the plastic sheeting. There were rats everywhere. The best they could do was shoo them away from the children.

By morning they were all exhausted. As the sun rose, they caught each other's eyes. This camp was completely different from the Burundi camps where they had been given housing. Here they were given nothing but plastic sheeting.

"Tufanye nini sasa?" the adults asked each other. "What do we do now?"

CHAPTER SEVENTY-SEVEN

You Can't Wait

Mapendo and Argentine slept out in the bush in those makeshift shelters for weeks. They didn't know what else to do. Other refugees had been granted plots of land to farm, way out in the bush. One day, Joseph's name was called.

"Follow me," the man had said to the refugees he had gathered. "I am going to take you to the land you have been assigned. You can farm there. Build a house there. We expect you to provide for yourselves."

The man marched off quickly over the hills, like a soldier, and disappeared. The other refugees followed him, but Joseph remained standing there, studying the hills. There was no way he could keep up with that march. For his family, there was simply nowhere to go.

Argentine, Mapendo, and Joseph kept waiting for the camp officials to return, for someone to check on them as they had been promised. They hoped, somehow, they would finally be seen. But, in this camp, no one was looking for them.

"You can't wait for help in this camp," another refugee told them. "You have to look out for yourselves. If you have any money, go and find somewhere to rent."

In a refugee camp, no one can afford to be penniless, especially not those who live with disabilities. Refugee camps have their own economies and their own hierarchies. Refugees who had arrived years prior lived on land close to the camp headquarters, near the health clinic, school and water supply. Newly arrived refugees found themselves on land far from any resources at all, including water. This dynamic was only made worse by Argentine, Mapendo, and Joseph's disabilities.

Joseph heard about a small hut for rent near the center of the camp. He went to look. He found a little shelter built nearly on top of another small hut. The shelter was being offered for rent by a refugee who had arrived in the camp years ago. In the entrepreneurial spirit of refugees everywhere, this man had considered his limited resources and built a rental property on the land he had been granted. This rental property was only a humble shelter, with a dirt floor and clay sides, but in the camp, it was a valuable commodity. Argentine, Mapendo, and Joseph paid the rent and moved in.

CHAPTER SEVENTY-EIGHT

Canada

Around that time, Elissa, one of our SHONA Congo customers, sent me a message. *I am in a refugee sponsorship group here in my small town in Canada. Maybe we can sponsor Argentine, Mapendo, and their families and bring them to Canada,* Elissa wrote.

The suggestion sounded impossible to me. In the camps, there were always rumors of those rare refugees who had been whisked away to a different future, to be resettled somewhere safe and permanent. But it was never clear how those few refugees might have gotten that opportunity. There were simply far too many refugees and far too few resettlement spaces.

I knew how low the chances were. I knew that, globally, the number of spaces available to resettle refugees reflected only a tiny fraction of the number of people who were forcibly displaced throughout the world.* I knew that most refugees and otherwise displaced people remained indefinitely in the locations where they had sought refuge, often living for years in refugee and IDP camps, or running in circles, just as Argentine and Mapendo had already done. On the run and in the camps, the

* For the year 2018, the UNHCR estimated that 1 in every 500 refugees was resettled.

quest for survival consumed all resources. Years spun together, with children often unable attend school and parents unable to work. Refugees existed in a precarious limbo that seemed to extend forever outward, with no hope of permanency in sight. Argentine had spent over two years in the refugee camp in Burundi and there was never any glimmer of permanent resettlement. Now, in Uganda, she and Mapendo felt more invisible than ever.

But here was this Canadian proposing that her community could sponsor them, specifically.

Could it be possible? In the United States we have no ability to identify and privately sponsor a specific refugee. But this Canadian seemed to believe it was possible there.

Was this the next step? And even if it was possible, was Canada the right future for them, far from the families they loved? I had serious doubts. But sitting in my apartment in New York, listening to stories of my friends battling mud, mosquitos and malaria, I knew that the choice wasn't mine to make.

CHAPTER SEVENTY-NINE

The Choice

"Of course we want to go to Canada!" Argentine and Mapendo exclaimed. I stumbled for words.

"It is really cold in Canada. It is really far away," I said.

"Is there war in Canada?" Mapendo asked.

"No," I answered.

"We want to go to Canada," she said with that steady voice of hers. I could picture a firm smile creeping across her broad face.

"But you will be far, far away from your families. You might never see them again," I said, thinking of Mapendo's mother in her hospital bed. I tried to communicate the loneliness and loss of identity that immigrants often face far from their families.

But Mapendo would have none of it.

"What can I do for my family from here?" she said. "They will be happy for us if we go to Canada."

I tried to tell Argentine and Mapendo that it was a long shot. The truth was I had absolutely no idea if we had any shot at all. But this, apparently, was the next step, a step that had materialized at our feet. We took it.

CHAPTER EIGHTY

What Makes a Refugee

Elissa introduced me to the Athabasca Interfaith Refugee Sponsorship Society (AIRSS). I learned that AIRSS was a small group of individuals in the rural town of Athabasca, in northern Alberta, Canada. The group had formed after an Athabasca resident asked members of his local church to help sponsor and resettle his family members who had fled Congo and were living in a refugee camp. In response to that request, the church formed a sponsorship group, and eventually AIRSS was formed as an outgrowth of that group. In 2012, three of the man's family members were resettled to Canada with AIRSS support.

In 2014, AIRSS sponsored a second family, this time a mother and son from Eritrea. Now, through a miracle that I couldn't quite understand, AIRSS was considering sponsoring Argentine, Mapendo, and their families.

I learned that Canada has a refugee sponsorship program that allows for private sponsorship. This program exists in addition to a government assisted resettlement program. The private sponsorship pathway allows community groups to use their own energy, and raise their own funds, to sponsor and resettle refugees within their own community. Amazingly, the program allows these community groups to submit the names of specific refugees that the group would like to sponsor. Since Argentine and Mapendo were registered by UNHCR in the refugee camp in Uganda, AIRSS could try to sponsor them specifically.

I had never imagined this type of program might exist. It had always felt like Argentine and Mapendo were lost in a sea of refugees. But now, because of this unique Canadian program, they were no longer invisible.

The process required AIRSS to submit sponsorship applications on behalf of each family. In addition, Argentine and Mapendo needed to complete applications for permanent residence in Canada for themselves and their families.

I started working with Kate, a member of AIRSS. Together we agreed to help the families complete their permanent residence applications. Kate was a law student, organized and determined. She was always interested in a new challenge. I am not sure if she knew what she was signing up for, but I know, for certain, that I had no idea.

Kate oversaw the permanent residence applications and organized all the information. It was an enormous undertaking. My task was to help the families fill out the applications, then pass the information on to Kate.

At first the task seemed manageable, until I started reading the directions, page after page. The main application was lengthy and there were additional schedules and background information that needed to be filled out as well. The words soon began to blur in my head.

**Provide the details of your personal history for the past ten years. Failure to account for every time period will result in delay of your application.*

**Describe the exact route of your journey to your present location, starting from your departure from your home country.*

**Set out in chronological order all the significant incidents that caused you to seek protection outside your home country.*

The application was in English. Argentine and Mapendo spoke Swahili. At first, I thought I could just translate the application into Swahili and ask my friends to write their responses. But the task quickly became overwhelming. My Congolese friends remembered their lives in a series of long narratives with very few dates. It was no small challenge to fit the narratives of their lives into the neat grids that the Canadian government sent, with columns labeled for the date and location.

Who, after all, can remember the details of life so specifically, even when not touched by trauma? Now, my friends were fighting for their lives in a refugee camp, trying to scare rats away from their sleeping children, and meanwhile trying to answer my questions about what they had been doing for the past ten years.

For refugees who have no formal education, who speak only a local language, and who have no outside connections, the process of applying for permanent residence in another country is almost impossible to navigate. The truth is that without an advocate on their behalf, our most vulnerable refugees are likely to remain unseen, lost in a process that they have no idea how to even begin.

Sitting in New York, I had somehow imagined all refugees as equal, arriving with only the clothes on their backs. But refugees arrive in camps with hugely disparate resources. Language, education, money, and above all, connections, are currencies that help the lucky few navigate the process and hold many others frozen in place.

I understood then the task that lay before us. These applications would only ever be filled out as a group project. Kate was researching the process and providing me with every part of the application that Argentine, Mapendo, and Joseph needed to respond to. She also sent lists of the supporting documentation that would be required.

In Uganda, Joseph scrambled to find every required document. The families had left Congo with every type of document they had in their possession—every birth certificate, every identity card, every official document they could find. But still there were gaps. Mapendo and Joseph's original marriage certificate had been lost. There were mistakes on official documents. Names were sometimes spelled differently. Joseph scanned the documents we had. Kate wrote letters to explain any discrepancies. And we hoped that whoever received these applications would understand why, for the average refugee, having all the right supporting documents can be an impossible hurdle.

As Joseph and Kate gathered supporting documents, Argentine, Mapendo, and I began trying to fill out the applications, painstakingly walking through the details of their lives over long distance phone calls.

I thought of our first phone calls when I moved back to New York, how I stumbled through Swahili, and Mapendo spoke so quickly. Now we had seven years of practice communicating over the phone. It was as though we had been preparing for this all along. I had kept a SHONA Congo blog over the previous ten years, and gradually we matched their memories to the details that were recorded in the blog. It took months to fill out the applications.

Always I circled around one question. *What makes a refugee?*

Was the seed of Argentine's refugee status planted the first time she fled Goma, with her fiancé pushing her along on the kinga? Or was it planted years before, when her family found that it was no longer safe to farm their land? Or maybe it was when the armed men broke down her door, shone flashlights in her face, and told her she was a good girl.

Or maybe it was years before all of that, when Argentine was only a small child, and she contracted polio. That was when she lost the ability to run, a prerequisite to life in eastern Congo.

To be honest, I don't know what made a refugee. I never did find the answer. But what I came to believe is that the path started long before anyone was looking. The conditions that made a country unlivable were not born in the events that made the news—when rebels took control of Goma, when the minerals in our cell phone became a hot topic, or when people on social media started calling eastern Congo the "rape capital of the world." What made eastern Congo unlivable for Mapendo and Argentine was the combination of their physical disabilities with the poverty and violence that frames everyday life in so many corners of our world.

Sitting on my porch, lost in thought, I struggled to finish the applications. *What does it mean to be a refugee? How could we communicate how intensely vulnerable each of these individuals was, while also capturing their power, dignity, and faith?*

I flipped through the long lists of questions, looking for one section that might offer some relief.

Finally, I found a prompt, tucked on the bottom of a page.

"Give examples of any work experience, skills, and/or personal qualities that would assist you in settling in Canada."

It wasn't exactly the topic I was looking for, but at least it was a start.

CHAPTER EIGHTY-ONE

Enough Spots

While Kate and I were helping Argentine, Mapendo, and Joseph to fill out the applications for permanent residence, the members of AIRSS were also working to complete their sponsorship applications.

AIRSS quickly ran into a problem. Like all countries, Canada cannot resettle an infinite number of refugees. The government sets a fixed number of spots available to refugees. The spots for the private sponsorship program are allocated to groups known as Sponsorship Agreement Holders (SAH). These SAH are incorporated organizations that sign a formal agreement with the Canadian government. They are generally large organizations that submit several refugee sponsorships per year. They also often partner with other smaller groups, like AIRSS, giving allocated spaces to them and authorizing them to sponsor refugees under their agreements.

When Cheryl, the president of AIRSS, contacted the SAH that they had previously worked with, she discovered that they had no available spots. It might be years before they had any. That was when Cheryl realized that amid the global refugee crisis the demand for allocated spots had sky-rocketed, leaving groups struggling to find any available spots.

The members of AIRSS found themselves staring at a blank wall. *How would they ever find the ten spots that they needed?*

AIRSS had no connections to any other SAH. The whole process of trying to find allocated spots was new to them. Still, they refused to give up. Members of AIRSS began making phone calls and writing emails. They were quickly told it was extremely rare to find any extra spots. They needed at least ten spots.

One day, Elissa made a follow-up phone call to Gail Millard, from the Anglican Diocese of Edmonton, a SAH. "They can give us six spots!" Elissa reported with excitement. This was progress.

But what would AIRSS do with six spots? How could they split up the families? How could they choose who to put first?

"Maybe I can find more spots. I'll see what I can do," Gail promised.

A few weeks later, Gail returned with a miracle. "I have found ten spots for you," she said. Relief flooded over the members of AIRSS.

Even with that hurdle crossed, there were still many more hurdles ahead. AIRSS had to raise funds to demonstrate that they could cover all the basic living expenses for both families in their first year in Canada. AIRSS estimated that amount to be at least Can$58,500 (US$44,000). Considering the needs of these two families, AIRSS knew they probably needed to raise more than the minimum.

When I first heard how much was needed, I nearly gave up. With SHONA, we had been grinding away for years for far smaller sums. AIRSS likewise had never had to raise so much money. But AIRSS was committed to continuing forward. They held fundraisers and reached out to the Athabasca community.

And the whole SHONA Congo community joined them. Donations arrived, large and small, from countless friends who had followed this journey for so long. When about half of the funds had been raised, an anonymous donor appeared. *Our family will donate whatever you still need to reach your goal,* that donor wrote to me. The message was from a longtime SHONA friend. Years ago, we had sewed some shirts and bags for her family. We had never imagined where that would one day lead. In countless ways it was as though the groundwork had been unknowingly laid for years.

In June of 2016, AIRSS submitted the permanent residence applications for both families along with the sponsorship applications. It was a huge relief to have made it that far. We celebrated that milestone—then we looked at the cold, hard numbers. The estimated processing time for their applications was seventy months—nearly six years.

Could Argentine, Mapendo, and their families survive in a refugee camp for another six years?

CHAPTER EIGHTY-TWO

Asante Mungu

June 2016

Life in the refugee camp went from bad to worse. A few months earlier, Argentine's fiancé had packed his things and left the refugee camp. His mother had been sick and his family in Congo had been calling him nearly every day, begging him to come home. Argentine sent him text messages in Congo, asking if he would come back to Uganda soon. But he never came back. Sometimes relationships explode. And sometimes they just slip away, like sand through our fingertips. Argentine's fiancé slipped away and never returned.

This left Argentine living alone with her sister Aline (age twelve). Men began to stop by Argentine's house. They asked where her fiancé was. They suggested she needed a man. Often, they were drunk.

Nearly every day Argentine wheeled herself to the health clinic in the wheelchair she had been given. She sat waiting all day to see a doctor. "Return tomorrow," she was told again and again.

The health clinic was bare bones, lacking even the most basic medicine and equipment. Argentine had been told that they conducted c-sections there, but it was hard to believe, when the clinic didn't even seem to have aspirin.

"Don't worry, everything will be fine. We will transfer you to the main hospital in Fort Portal when your date gets closer," a doctor finally promised.

Fort Portal was a city, seventy-five kilometers (fifty-two miles) away, over bumpy roads. What would happen if Argentine went into labor unexpectedly?

"Let's just send Argentine to Fort Portal ourselves. We can pay for the hospital," I suggested over the phone.

I had forgotten what it means to be a refugee. As a refugee, every decision required permission from authorities.

Mapendo began waking at dawn and waiting outside of the camp offices in a mixture of determination and desperation. She sat there in long lines. She waited and waited. Sometimes she brought Jonathan and Joachim, and sometimes she left them behind.

"Please, give us permission to move to Fort Portal," she begged. "We will pay for our own housing. We will pay for the hospital for Argentine. We can't survive here."

"These decisions can't be made just like that. Come back another day," the officials responded.

Day after day, Mapendo was told, "Come back tomorrow."

I began to despair. "Just leave the camp! Go to Fort Portal!" I would sometimes exclaim in exasperation. But Mapendo and Argentine insisted that they could not leave the camp without permission.

The members of AIRSS agreed to send an urgent email on Argentine's behalf, asking for immediate medical care.

The next day Argentine heard knocking at her door. She opened the door and couldn't believe her eyes. The camp doctor was standing on her doorstep. She had spent months in the clinic begging to see a doctor, and now he was standing before her. The doctor told Argentine that he would accompany her to the Fort Portal Hospital himself. A few days later, they went. Argentine traveled with the doctor in a van full of refugees being transferred to the hospital. But when they got to the hospital, Argentine's heart sank as she saw the conditions. The hospital was packed with refugees and other desperate-looking patients. The doctor took one look around and ordered Argentine back onto the minibus. He brought Argentine to a small Catholic hospital nearby.

When Argentine arrived on the peaceful grounds of the Catholic hospital, she began to breathe again. The nuns welcomed her. Argentine couldn't understand their words, but their smiles were warm. The Catholic doctor agreed to schedule a c-section for Argentine for the following week. And, for a minute, it all seemed okay.

Then the camp doctor abruptly entered the room. "Let's go," he said, urging Argentine to pack her things. "We have to get back to the camp." Argentine grabbed her belly and imagined riding the seventy-five kilometers over bumpy roads back to the camp.

But before she could even stand, the staff at the Catholic hospital surrounded her. "Why would you take a woman in this condition back to the camp?" the Catholic doctor exclaimed. He refused to let Argentine go, even if it meant that the UNHCR would not pay the bill. The nuns gave Argentine a private room with a view onto a flowering courtyard. "We'll find the funding later," they promised.

Argentine slept well that night, remembering years before, the first time she had met a nun, offering her porridge and a safe place to sleep on that night she had first arrived in Goma.

Argentine's daughter was born a week later, surrounded by strangers who had chosen to welcome a pregnant refugee. Argentine named her daughter "Asante Mungu." Her name means "Thank You God."

CHAPTER EIGHTY-THREE

Impermanence

August 2016

Back in the refugee camp, Mapendo and Joseph had continued their vigil at the camp offices, still asking for permission for their family and Argentine's family to move to Fort Portal, where they could be closer to medical care and where it would be easier for them to begin to sew again. One day, as Mapendo and Joseph sat in line, they caught sight of an official slipping out a side door to smoke. Mapendo stood, determined. "I am going after him," she whispered to Joseph. She leaned on her crutches and followed the official outside. "Nihurumie," she said. "Have mercy on me," She begged for help that day. A few weeks later, after a few more meetings, they received permission to move to Fort Portal.

When Argentine, Mapendo, and Joseph left the refugee camp they promised they would provide for themselves. Joseph set about looking for a house to rent in Fort Portal. He found a compound with two small houses for rent, side by side. It was perfect. He paid the advance. But a day later something went wrong. The landlord returned the money. "We can't rent to families like yours. You're refugees. There are so many of you," he mumbled. They found another house and moved in happily, but a few months later someone started throwing rocks at the house. It was never clear who was throwing the rocks or why. It was just one more reminder that they were foreigners in someone else's land. They registered Aline, Ziada and Jonathan for school, but the schools were taught in English and the older girls found it difficult to adjust with little support. Argentine found a church that she loved where she was welcomed and given the opportunity to sing. Some people were kind, and some people were not, but always they were aware that they were strangers in a foreign land.

As always, Argentine and Mapendo were determined to continue sewing. They went to the market and bought cloth, pointing at colors and using the few words they knew in the local language. They sewed bags. Then they wrapped up the bundle of SHONA bags and traveled 300 kilometers (186 miles) to the capital city of Kampala to ship the bags, navigating another new city and another new language.

They sewed proudly. But they lived as refugees—always unsure of the shifting ground under their feet and always prepared to flee again.

CHAPTER EIGHTY-FOUR

The Crucial Step

August 2017

Eighteen months after they first arrived in Uganda, Joseph and Mapendo were informed that they had been scheduled for an interview with the Canadian government.

Amazingly, Argentine was scheduled for an interview on the exact same day.

We could feel the whole world turning. It felt like a miracle. Maybe it was.

An interview was the crucial step. We had been told that if they ever were called for an interview, the chances were high that they would be accepted. But still, you never know. Applicants were sometimes rejected after an interview when the stories of their lives didn't hold together or when more documentation was needed.

"Just tell them the truth," I said confidently. "Everything on that application is the truth." And it was. But still, every story depends on who tells it, and how. We hoped the translator would be good.

The preparation materials for the interview explained that if you missed your interview, that was the end of the road. You would not be considered a second time.

Argentine, Mapendo, and Joseph had been instructed to go to an office in Kampala on September 7, 2017. They had to navigate an unfamiliar city, in a language they didn't know. They needed to bring all six children. They were to arrive at 8:00 AM, and they couldn't be late.

My mind swarmed with the possibilities for disaster.

What if one of the children was sick? Someone was always sick.

What if they got lost in Kampala? Just recently Mapendo and Joseph had been traumatized by a trip to Kampala. They had gone to the city to send bags to me. After leaving the post office, they had called to a motorcycle taxi and climbed aboard, instructing him to take them to a hotel. They knew where the hotel was. It was nearby. But the motorcycle taxi driver could tell they were not from Uganda. He had driven them in circles until they no longer knew where they were. They started to notice signs for the outskirts of the city.

"Let us down right here!" Joseph had shouted, his heart thumping. He had been warned about unscrupulous taxi drivers. They would drive foreigners out to vacant areas, beat them, and steal all their money. "Let us down NOW," Joseph shouted again, thankful the road was still crowded with people.

"But we aren't there yet," the driver responded, "just be patient."

"No! You are trying to make us lost! Stop now!" Joseph shouted. Finally, the driver had stopped.

This time, for the interview, they could afford no mistakes and no bad luck. Everything had to go right.

CHAPTER EIGHTY-FIVE

The Interview

September 2017

Argentine, Mapendo, Joseph, and their families arrived in Kampala two days early. This gave them time to find a hotel and scout out the office in advance. The day before the interview, Joseph went to the office to confirm the location. He walked into the building and asked, "Is this the right place for the interview with the Canadian government?" It was a question he had never imagined having the opportunity to ask.

"This is the place," he was told.

The next morning, they woke at dawn. Their families were the first to arrive at the office. As the sun rose, the crowd grew longer and longer behind them, waiting for the doors to open.

Finally, they were invited inside.

Argentine walked in for her interview, leaning on her crutches and throwing her legs forward as she always did. She looked up from her crutches and was surprised to find two women inside, sitting behind a desk. She saw their kind faces and breathed a sigh of relief.

They invited Argentine to sit down.

"What a beautiful dress you have on," one of the women said.

"I sewed it myself," Argentine replied proudly.

The woman broke into a grin. "You made this yourself," the woman echoed back, reaching her hand toward the vibrantly colored cloth and shaking her head in wonder. "It's beautiful," the woman whispered. "Maybe you will sew a dress for me someday."

CHAPTER EIGHTY-SIX

At the Airport

December 2017

Three months later I stood in the Edmonton International Airport waiting for Argentine and Mapendo to arrive. My stomach churned. How was it possible that now, after all these years, I would see my friends again? And how was it possible that our reunion would take place under the fluorescent lights of an airport in northwestern Canada, a place none of us had ever imagined?

On the day I left, nearly nine years earlier, we had sat on the green grass at the shores of Lake Kivu. We had drunk Fanta together while looking out at the lake. Argentine and Mapendo had told stories of their fears of the water, of drowning in the shimmering lake. Then they had laughed and laughed, as if to hide all our fears.

"Usitusahau," they said. "Don't forget us."

"Sitakusahau," I replied. "I will not forget you."

It was the refrain of Congo.

My husband and I got in a vehicle borrowed from work, and we climbed the green terraced hills back into the heart of Rwanda. Congo got farther and farther away.

Soon, we arrived back in Kigali, the capital city of Rwanda. I was violently sick. Malaria had captured my body. My skin was burning, and my shoulders ached. I retreated to a hotel bed, and the world faded into a daze.

Three years earlier, when we had first arrived in Congo and stayed at the desolate, beautiful Hotel Karibu, I had also gotten terribly sick, retreating into a hotel bed until my body no longer felt like my own. And then one day I had awoken from the fog of my sickness. "We must find a place to live," I had said. I spent the next three years finding a place to live—a way to live—in the city of Goma.

Now, nine years later, I stood in an airport in Canada trying to imagine how my friends would do the same in this frozen place. How would they find a place to live, and a way to live, in this country they could barely imagine?

At 7 PM a plane from Toronto was expected to touch down, completing Argentine, Mapendo, and their families' two-day journey from Uganda to Canada. I stood at the airport next to Kate. Over the past year we had worked together for countless hours on the phone, completing each individual application. But I had never actually met Kate face-to-face before. Still, I knew why she was there. I knew that Kate had joined AIRSS only shortly before we began to work on the applications. She joined AIRSS because every day she would drive a long commute to law school and listen to the news. The state of the world became too much to bear. She joined AIRSS because she wanted to do something tangible—one small thing that might make the world just a little bit better.

Kate and I stood with a few members of AIRSS and a seemingly random collection of other people. Elissa was there, the SHONA customer who had first dared this dream. Gail Millard was there, the woman from the SAH who had miraculously found enough spots. Someone had come to take pictures. Someone else had brought her daughter, adopted from Congo a few years earlier.

We stood there as a welcoming committee, strangers even among ourselves. But we were not really strangers. The act of coming together to welcome others had transformed us into a community, as though the intention held some healing power, long before any plane touched down.

We stood there for a long time, in the arrivals section of the airport. Someone had made welcome signs. The sliding doors whooshed open and we jumped up, welcome signs flashing. My heart fell to my stomach. Strangers walked through the doors. But Argentine and Mapendo were nowhere to be seen. After a while, the sliding doors stopped opening. It seemed like all the passengers had already arrived.

What if they weren't coming after all? My stomach was in knots. What if, after all of this, they had gotten lost somewhere along the way?

Finally, the elevator doors slid open behind us.

Joseph arrived, smiling and shaking hands with everyone in sight. Neema and Ziada and the two little boys arrived. Neema and Ziada were dressed in athletic track suits, hoods pulled up. I was thrown off by their clothing—they looked like they might have come from New York City. But then I looked past the tracksuits and saw something else. These two teenage girls were walking up to everyone with their arms outstretched. They were hugging and thanking everyone they saw, trusting themselves into the arms of strangers. There was something about the way that they greeted everyone—an openness—it carried another world with them.

Mapendo rolled out in a wheelchair. Her broad face smiled out from underneath warm clothing. In all my time in Congo, I had never seen her in a wheelchair before. She rolled forward, then she stood, steadying herself as she reached for her crutches. Then she wrapped me into her arms. “Dada, dada,” she repeated, and it felt like she would never let go.

Finally, Argentine and Aline arrived along with Asante Mungu.

Argentine was in a wheelchair, and I saw her before she saw me. Sitting low in her wheelchair, without her metal leg braces on, I knew she couldn’t stand up. Instead, she was pulling each person toward her.

Finally, she saw me. “Dada,” she said.

“Siku nyingi,” I said. “Many days...”

“Siku nyingi kabisa.” “So many days,” Argentine answered.

Swahili suddenly stuck in my throat. What could I possibly say after a journey that was nearly nine years long? I leaned down and hugged Argentine. She pulled me in, and I didn’t dare let go.

PART III

CHAPTER EIGHTY-SEVEN

The Road to Athabasca

December 2017

On the trip from the airport to Athabasca, I rode in the car with Argentine. Athabasca is a small town about two hours from the larger city of Edmonton. I had never been to Athabasca. Neither Argentine nor I knew what to expect. We nibbled on the cheese and crackers that Elissa had brought along and chatted in Swahili in the backseat. I asked Argentine and Aline if they liked the flavors of the food.

"Butamu sana." "Very delicious," Argentine said with a white-toothed smile. I was sure that she would have given the same response no matter what we had offered her.

Argentine said that the airplane food had been terrible. Everything was sweet. And Asante Mungu had been sick the entire way. Argentine was petrified on each of their three airplane rides. And exhausted.

But still, tucked into this warm car, driving off into the darkness of rural Canada, Argentine seemed perfectly at home and full of life. I thought of all my concerns about life in Canada and about how Argentine would find community here. Looking at

Argentine in the car, her face shining with enthusiasm, her hand reaching out to grab my arm, I wondered what I had been so worried about. *Argentine will make friends anywhere,* I told myself, looking at her smiling face.

As we approached Athabasca, we couldn't see much outside, only the shadows of trees. I saw Argentine peering out the car window at the empty road before her. She remained silent for a while.

"Dada," she finally said, "where are all the people?"

The roads in Goma are crowded with people. This was December in a rural town in Canada, and the roads were entirely empty.

CHAPTER EIGHTY-EIGHT

What They Carried

On that warm car ride to Athabasca, Argentine told me about their last few months in Africa. They had gone to the interview in Kampala. "We'll call you to discuss the next steps," the Canadian officials had promised through a translator.

I asked Argentine if she had been nervous after the interview, in the months between the interview and the final acceptance, in those moments of unknowing.

"Haukuogopa?" "Weren't you afraid?" I asked.

"Sikuogopa hata." "I wasn't afraid at all," she said. Then she turned to me and continued, "I knew God would take care of us. I knew we would make it."

She spoke in a voice full of confidence. I pictured her at the beginning of this journey, as a child under that tree with the snakes. "We have to go now," she had told her mother in the voice of a prophet. She'd been right both times.

"What happened when you were finally accepted?" I asked.

"Well," Argentine began, "we went for the interview in September. In October we were called back to Kampala for medical screenings. In November, we were issued visas. That is when it became real."

I sat there in the car with Argentine, chatting in Swahili and staring at the lights on the road up ahead. Snow stretched out on every side of us. She told me how she called her mother and begged her to come to Uganda to say goodbye. "Borrow the money, do whatever you have to, just please come before it is too late," she had said to her mother.

Argentine's mother came, from Kitchanga to Goma, then traveling the road to Bunagana, tracing her daughter's footsteps in a country that was never safe enough. She came to say goodbye to not one, but two of her daughters: Argentine and Aline, her second youngest child, now thirteen years old.

Mapendo's mother was too sick to come, and Mapendo's heart broke, thinking of her mother in a hospital bed in Goma. *I wish I could have brought her with me*, she thought, not for the first time.

Mapendo's sister came instead. By this point, Neema and Ziada had lived with Mapendo for many years, but this was still their mother, always their mother. She came to hug her daughters goodbye before they disappeared over an invisible line.

"Usininihau." "Don't forget me," their mother probably said.

"Hatutakusahau." They would have responded. "We won't forget you."

Joseph talked on the phone to his father, who was struggling to find money to buy a bus ticket to Uganda.

"I have visited everyone in our village, and no one has money to lend to me," his father had said.

"Don't worry Papa. Stay home where you are safe. God will protect us," Joseph responded.

But his father was determined to see them before they left Uganda. Only nine months earlier, Joseph's mother had died. And now his father was desperate to say goodbye to a son he knew he might never see again. He left the village and began to walk. He walked over one hundred kilometers (sixty-two miles) along the lake, the same route that Joseph had fled years earlier, in the opposite direction. Finally, he arrived in Goma, where he found someone to lend him the money for a bus ticket to Uganda.

"I'm coming. I'm coming," he told Joseph over the phone.

A few days later, Joseph went to the bus depot in Fort Portal to meet his father. It was the first time he had seen his father since his mother died. Just as the two men fell into each other's arms, Joseph's cell phone began to ring. Joseph answered the phone, still standing there in the parking lot holding his father's hand. A voice on the other end of the line told Joseph that they needed to prepare to leave immediately. They were needed in Kampala the very next day.

Time telescoped. Their flight was not for another week. They thought they had that week to spend with their family, to pack their things, to say goodbye to an entire continent. But with a simple phone call, everything changed. They were refugees, dependent on the whims of a system they couldn't fully understand. They had to follow instructions. They had to be prepared to leave at the drop of a hat.

They had less than an hour to pack up their lives in Fort Portal, and then they had to find a ride to the refugee camp, nearly eighty kilometers (fifty miles) away. The next morning, they would be on a bus from the camp to Kampala. In Kampala they would attend a resettlement orientation program. They would not return to Fort Portal. Whatever they left behind, would stay behind.

Joseph stood there in that parking lot, his heart suddenly wrenched in two. "Don't cry, my son," his father said, his sandals still dusty from the long journey. "God brought me here. God gave us the chance to see each other again."

Joseph called Mapendo at the house. "Pack whatever you can. We have to be ready to leave in half an hour," he said.

Mapendo stared at her life spread out before her. There were clothes that were waiting to be washed. There was food they had been planning to eat.

There wasn't enough time to think about what to pack. They had no bags to pack anything. Mapendo bundled clothing inside an African cloth and tied it closed.

When Joseph and his father arrived at the house, he sent for someone to buy oil. Then he anointed his grandsons with oil, gently touching their shoulders, conjuring up a future he would never see.

"God bless you. And God bless the people who will welcome you," he said. Then he paused and whispered the refrain of Congo. "Usinisahau." "Don't forget me."

They left the house. Joseph's father and Argentine's mother accompanied them back to the refugee camp, hanging onto each last minute with their children and grandchildren.

But by the time they reached the refugee camp that night, it was late and there was no more time for talking. The next morning Argentine, Mapendo, Joseph, and all the children climbed on a minibus. They waved goodbye and turned their faces toward the future once again.

In Kampala, they were admitted into a facility where refugees were gathered before resettlement. Once they entered, they were not permitted to leave again. They attended orientation. They were told to buy suitcases and warm clothing for the children. They called Argentine's brother who was staying nearby and asked him to buy those things. He brought track suits and sneakers for the children and big empty suitcases to pack their things in.

Mapendo folded little boy clothes, and African fabric, but everything they owned didn't fill the suitcase and it rattled around half empty. Other refugees had arrived at the compound looking shiny and fresh to Argentine and Mapendo's eyes, with suitcases stuffed full. Argentine and Mapendo looked at their suitcases regretfully, wishing they had more to carry with them. Then they zipped the bags shut.

For all their travels, they had always watched their bags being tied onto the roof of a bus or piled underneath them on a truck. But when they arrived at the airport, their suitcases simply disappeared behind a wall. Joseph stood there in the airport staring after the suitcases, watching all their remaining possessions disappear from sight. *Where will those bags end up?* He wondered. *Will we ever see them again?*

Finally, the families were taken to a gate, and they boarded the airplane. And then another airplane. And then another airplane, until they could no longer count all the airplanes that had carried them into the sky.

After more than twenty hours of travel, they arrived in Edmonton airport. They were escorted through the airport, and finally they entered the elevator. The doors to the elevator slid open and we embraced under the fluorescent lights.

"Let's get your luggage," someone in our group finally said, and we walked to the carousel nearby. And there, miraculously, were their black and brown suitcases, carried in circles on a strange rubber belt.

CHAPTER EIGHTY-NINE

All Things New

When we arrived in Athabasca that night, we went to the Athabasca Reformed Church Ministry Center which was providing temporary housing for the families until permanent housing could be arranged. The facility had previously been used for senior housing, and it was perfect, with private rooms, a communal kitchen, and wheelchair accessibility.

Volunteers from AIRSS and from the church had prepared the rooms. Glittery welcome signs hung in each room. There were toys for the children to play with, and Elissa had arranged bins with clothing in every size. A kind woman from the church took us on a tour of the facility and asked me to translate.

"This is where the microwave is," she said, pointing to her right.

"Unaweza chamusha chakula hapa," I said, opting for a loose translation. "You can heat food here." Then I looked doubtfully at the microwave, a machine with twenty or so buttons on it. *Maybe I can explain more later*, I thought to myself. Our tour had already moved on to the next room.

"Here is the laundry room. To wash the clothes, you just pull this dial and twist it like this. Select the size of your wash, then..."

"Uhm...this thing is for washing clothes," I said in Swahili to Aline, Ziada, and Neema, picturing the years they had spent squatting on the ground over a plastic basin, scrubbing clothes by hand.

Argentine and Mapendo had fallen back to the edge of our group, fussing with children and navigating wheelchairs. But the teenage girls stared into the washing machine, fascinated. They opened the door to the dryer. "Wait, what do we do again?" they asked me in Swahili.

In those first days it was the girls who struck me most. I could see their lives suddenly taking a sharp turn. Neema had not attended school for over six years. Now she would be starting eighth grade in Athabasca.

The girls tried on clothes that came out of the plastic bins. How do I look in this?" they asked one another, giggling.

On one of those first days, Kate came over to the facility, carrying bundles of board games. She dressed all the children in warm clothing. "Who wants to go outside?" she asked in French, hoping that language would be more familiar. Everyone looked at her with confusion. She pointed to the door and mimed playing in the snow.

The children's faces lit up. They clambered behind her, bundled in snow pants, boots, and mittens, more clothing than they had ever worn in their lives. Argentine and Mapendo in their wheelchairs followed too, twisting the wheels of the wheelchairs into the snow.

Argentine reached down and touched the snow for the first time. She threw her head back and laughed. Then with a glint in her eye, she started to form a snowball, just like the children were doing on the other side of the parking lot. The snow crumbled in her hands. She didn't yet know how to pack a snowball. Kate's son came over and pounded the snow down into a giant ball. "Here you go," he said in English, handing the snowball back to Argentine. Argentine aimed, then launched the snowball into the air. It sailed forward a couple feet. On the wings of success, Argentine gathered another handful of snow, packing it down this time. I stood nearby with my phone. "Argentine, look at me!" I called out, trying to capture the moment on video. Argentine looked into my eyes, flashed her white-toothed smile, then threw the snowball at me.

CHAPTER NINETY

Under the Snow

The next day, Gail Leicht, one of the AIRSS members, came by in her car. Mapendo climbed into the front seat. Argentine, Joseph, and I squished in the back. Gail drove us around Athabasca introducing us to the area.

"This is where Jonathan will go to school."

"This is the grocery store."

"Over there is the Catholic church."

I translated Gail's descriptions into Swahili. Argentine, Mapendo, and Joseph nodded and smiled at everything. When we passed by a series of modest bungalow-style houses, Joseph seemed captivated by the roofs.

"Is that snow on the roof?" he asked me in Swahili.

"Oh yes, that is snow," I confirmed, gesturing to the snow-covered lawns and trees.

But his eyes never moved from the roof. "But what is underneath the snow?"

"A roof!" I proclaimed. Then I paused thinking of those first pictures I had seen of Goma, the rows of white plastic tents in the IDP (Internally Displaced People) camps at the end of town. The snow-covered roofs looked strangely similar to the plastic tarps used in refugee and IDP camps.

Joseph was quietly checking that underneath all that snow, there was a solid roof, not one built out of plastic sheeting.

We circled the downtown area several times on our tour. I was pointing out a playground to Mapendo and talking about summer, when I finally glanced at the large expanse of snow beyond the playground.

"Wait," I said, pointing at the undisturbed snow, "Is that a river under the snow?"

"Oh, yes," Gail said, cheerfully.

I suppose she had thought it unnecessary to point out the river. Athabasca lies in a valley with a large, beautiful river coursing through the center of town. Everyone in Athabasca knows where the river is, even when it is covered with snow. It is there, always.

But my eyes were fresh, and I was a foreigner. Like Joseph with the roof, my eyes could not yet imagine what was hidden underneath the snow.

CHAPTER NINETY-ONE

Smoke

After a few days, I prepared to return to New York. I had a job and had only been able to take a few days off. "Why did you come for so few days?" Mapendo wanted to know in Swahili, her steady voice half-reproach and half invitation.

I hugged Mapendo goodbye, releasing her into a world she couldn't imagine. As I walked away from the church facility, I heard the doors click shut behind me. The church facility was equipped with automatically locking doors. The front door had a keypad with a code to enter. I had watched all my friends carefully memorizing the four-digit code. They practiced touching each button, then hitting enter, delighting as the door magically clicked open. I had also pointed at the smoke alarms in every room. I had tried to explain that the alarm would beep if there was a fire. But in each room, there was also a separate alarm that warned when water was overflowing in the bathroom. I probably didn't explain the alarms well. I couldn't find enough words to explain this new world where there was an alarm for every possible danger. I thought of the people of Goma, caught between one danger and another, without any alarms at all.

A few weeks after I left, the smoke alarm in the church facility went off. It was evening. The girls had been cooking, and the smoke detector began a shrill beeping sound. There was no fire, just smoke from the cooking.

But they didn't know that. The smoke alarm was loud and insistent, and it frightened them as they sat around the communal kitchen.

Emergency! they thought with pulses racing. *War*, Mapendo thought. She flew to her feet, grabbing her metal crutches. They all rushed out the back door. It clicked shut behind them.

Only after the door clicked shut did Mapendo start to breathe again. She made sure everyone was okay. The boys were safe. The girls were safe. Then she looked down. She was standing on the snow in her bare feet. It was December in Canada. "I can't feel my feet," Mapendo started to say.

Joseph called Kate at home, describing the emergency in French. She grabbed her keys and rushed into her car.

In the meantime, Mapendo stared at her feet, the sensation of cold still shockingly new. The back door to the church could not be opened from the outside. The only way back into the facility was all the way around the building, through the darkness and snow to the front entrance. They all began to walk, Mapendo's feet crunching on the icy snow.

A few minutes later, Kate's car flew into the parking lot of the church facility. "Come, come!" she called out, looking nervously at the small children shivering with cold and then at Mapendo's bare feet. They piled into the warmth of Kate's car. Someone from the church had arrived. He turned the alarm off and began checking the building. Soon, he gave the signal that the building was safe. They climbed back out of Kate's car and walked inside. When they arrived inside, Kate kneeled at Mapendo's feet. She warmed them gently and checked them for frostbite.

When Mapendo told me this story on the phone the next day, her voice was still filled with wonder at what she had survived. I thought she was surprised at the coldness of Canada. I knew it was colder than she could have ever imagined.

I asked Mapendo again, “Are you still happy to be in Canada?”

“Ndiyo, dada.” “Yes, sister,” she said in that steady voice, without hesitation.

“But isn’t it cold?” I asked pressing her further.

“Yes. But there is no war here—we raced outside and there was nothing—just silence.”

I heard that note of wonder in her voice again, and it finally occurred to me that it wasn’t the barefoot cold that had shocked Mapendo the most. It was silence of winter in Canada.

CHAPTER NINETY-TWO

Together

Gail Leicht, with her cheerful, can-do attitude, was in charge of helping the families find housing. "We want to live in two separate houses. But near each other, so we can still work together," Argentine and Mapendo tried to communicate in a mixture of French, Swahili, and hand gestures. Beyond the language challenges, they had no idea how difficult their request was.

Athabasca is a small town, and there aren't that many rental homes.

"We found two houses for rent on the same block," Gail finally reported. "We're lucky to find them!"

Gail took Mapendo, Joseph, and Argentine to visit the houses. "Haitawezekana," they reported back to me in Swahili. "It will not be possible. The houses are so far apart! We would never be able to visit each other!"

Argentine and Mapendo were used to the crowded-in construction of refugee camps and the shacks built nearly on top of each other in Goma. They were used to the safety of neighbors nearby, where cries of "tuko macho" could be heard in the night.

In Athabasca, houses have front yards and back yards. The sidewalk meanders and fills with snow in the winter. To

Argentine and Mapendo, "down the block" was still a world away. I wondered how they would ever keep hold of each other in this snowy place.

Thanks to persistence and good luck, AIRSS eventually found an apartment building on the far side of town with an elevator that could carry their wheelchairs, and with two apartments that would become vacant in the next several months.

Argentine and Mapendo moved into those two apartments, and brought with them their Congolese sense of community, with children running back and forth between the two apartments and all of them sharing meals.

When I next visited Canada, I delighted at the community that had formed. To my eyes, Argentine and Mapendo's apartments looked like a tiny village, always full of visitors. Cheryl stopped by to say hello. She brought baked goods to taste, and the boys ran up to hug her. Another Canadian friend rushed into Mapendo's apartment. She spoke English a mile a minute and handed out stacks of whole, frozen fish to the families. The language of food and generosity spoke for itself.

"Thank you, Sister!" Mapendo called out in English, still tentatively finding her voice in a new language.

Sitting in Mapendo's kitchen, I marveled at the generosity of the people of Athabasca, and the community that had formed around these two families. I also marveled at the way that Argentine and Mapendo had flipped the script just a bit. It was not always possible to tell exactly who was welcoming whom. Their apartments had become a stopping-by place, where everyone was equally welcomed, just as I had been welcomed in Congo many years before.

Sitting in Mapendo's apartment, I watched one of the neighbors, a middle-age woman, come in and out. Mapendo said that the woman visited often but rarely spoke. Occasionally, she disappeared and returned with the offer of an extra needle or thread. Then another neighbor arrived. He was a talkative gentleman who lived alone. He chatted with Joseph, then Joseph offered him dinner. “Sure, I can eat,” the older man said, sitting down at the table. We all ate, and Mapendo looked satisfied.

CHAPTER NINETY-THREE

Pancakes

One day, sitting at the kitchen table, I asked Aline what it was like to start school in Canada. Aline jumped in the air, always happy to launch into a story. She told me how on that first day, she followed a schedule the school had set for her—English...Science...Math. Toward the end of the day, the bell rang, and Social Studies ended. Aline followed the other students back toward homeroom. *It must be the end of the day,* Aline thought to herself. She walked into her homeroom.

"Time to go home?" Aline asked her teacher, piecing together words in English.

"Oh no, there is one more period," he answered.

Aline stared at her teacher.

"Sit down for a minute," the teacher said. "This is the Options period. You have a choice of classes."

Aline sat in her chair at the desk, thinking about the strange words spilled out before her—options, choices. The words swam in her head.

After a few minutes, the teacher reappeared. He leaned down next to Aline's desk, and looked at her gently through his glasses. "Aline, what do you like to do?"

The question floated into the air, then settled into Aline's brain. *What do I like to do?* she thought to herself.

"Do you like to cook?" the teacher asked.

"Cook?!? Yes! I like to cook," Aline responded, always enthusiastic.

"Maybe you will like the cooking class. Come with me," he said.

That first day in the school kitchen, Aline learned how to bake homemade buns. Later she learned to make spaghetti sauce and pancakes. Back at home, Aline proudly reported to Argentine that she was attending cooking class. Argentine burst out laughing.

"I sent you to school to learn...to *cook*?" Argentine exclaimed in disbelief. Aline had been cooking over a charcoal fire at home all her life.

What do they teach children at home if they teach them to cook at school? Argentine wondered. Then she shrugged her shoulders.

"It could be good," she said. "These Canadians, they must know what they are doing."

Aline was smitten with her new cooking class. "I LOVE Canadian food," she exclaimed. "I don't ever want to eat beans and potatoes again!"

When I came to visit Argentine, the first meal Aline cooked was spaghetti. The next morning, she made pancakes, struggling only a little to flip each one. When Aline proudly served up the pancakes, Argentine and Mapendo exchanged glances, shooing away the sticky sweet maple syrup.

"Too much sugar," Argentine said.

But Aline and Ziada sat down proudly at the table with a plate of pancakes between them, taste testing the difference between real maple syrup and fake.

"If we eat too many of these, we will get fat," Ziada said in English, a smile on her face. The two teenage girls burst out laughing. And then they settled down, savoring each bite, delighting in the sugary sweetness of life in Canada.

CHAPTER NINETY-FOUR

Make Me Cry

One afternoon, after the families had been in Athabasca a while, I walked from Mapendo's apartment, down the walkway towards Argentine's apartment. Before I ever reached Argentine's door, I could hear Aline's voice soaring. I pulled open the door and there was Aline, standing in the small living room singing.

There's always gonna be another mountain
I'm always gonna wanna make it move...

The only other person in the apartment was Ziada, but Aline's eyes were shut, her body moving up and down to the beat as though she were pumping up a crowd with her song.

Always gonna be an uphill battle
Sometimes I'm gonna have to lose
Ain't about how fast I get there
Ain't about what's waiting on the other side
It's the climb...

On the last word Aline threw her head back, abandoning herself to the song. Then she and Ziada clapped and the two girls collapsed into laughter.

"Okay, okay...my turn," Ziada said, serious again. She changed the music on the computer and started a new song...her voice rang out low and rich.

You don't have to change a thing.
The world could change its heart.
No scars to your beautiful.
We're stars and we're beautiful.

Ziada looked up at me mid-song, interrupting her own performance. "I sang this for the Battle of the Bands at school. But I had to stop part way through. I started crying," she confessed. "There is this part that always makes me cry..."

I turned my head quickly to look at Ziada, knowing that she has a beautiful voice and hoping she hadn't given up singing. I expected to see a tearful expression on Ziada's face. But instead she was smiling brightly, and her eyes were lit up with plans.

"I can't wait until next year," she said without skipping a beat. "Next year I am going to choose a song that doesn't make me cry."

In between Aline and Ziada's songs, they told me stories from school. They loved school, and they had good friends and supportive teachers. But still, Aline, Ziada, and Neema's lives existed in a minefield of sorts.

"There is this boy who says we're the poorest people in the town. He says we should go back to Africa," the girls confessed, lowering their voices to a whisper. Then they tilted their heads up and redirected the conversation, collectively choosing a song that didn't make them cry.

"I'm paying for my little brothers and my little sisters to go to school in Congo," Neema said proudly.

Neema works at the local grocery store after school, a place lit up with more lights and food than she could have ever imagined in Congo. She uses some of her paycheck to pay for life in Canada and some of it to pay for school fees for siblings in Congo, trying to undo an injustice that the world refuses to fix. Neema lives on this invisible line, the line between poverty and privilege. She is immensely grateful for the opportunity to go to school in Canada. She's equally thankful for the opportunity to work and send her siblings to school. Still, even with her help, Neema knows that her mother and siblings will struggle just to survive in Goma. The world is unfair.

I think back to Goma, and the lava rock walls with purple flowers hiding the razor wire. I think of my comfortable house with the white tile floors, and Mama Kavira with no floor at all.

This is the line that our world is facing, and it is only getting bigger with time, as the wealth gap grows, and record numbers of our world's population are displaced. I see Aline, Ziada and Neema poised with their toes pressed to the edge of this line, trying their best to hold it all together—to make sense of a world that offers vastly different futures to some of its children than to others. It is a responsibility too big for them to bear alone. It is one that belongs to all of us.

CHAPTER NINETY-FIVE

What it is Really Like

While writing this book, I read these stories back to Neema, Ziada, and Aline. "Do you want me to put this story in the book?" I asked.

"Yes. We want to be in the book," they all said.

I looked at Neema and Ziada. "Are you sure you want me to include this part about your father's death? If I write it in the book, people will ask you about it. Maybe it is something you don't want to talk about."

They looked at me carefully. "But that is the way it happened. We have to tell people what happened," they said.

"Is there anything else that you want me to include in this book?" I asked Aline and Ziada later that evening. Aline studied me.

"Did you really explain what it is like to live in Congo?"

I stared back at Aline. In the end, her Congo can never be mine. I will never do justice to the life she has lived.

"Well...probably not," I stammered. "What was it like?"

Aline and Ziada began to talk, as though they had been waiting for this opportunity all their lives.

"In Congo, we were the ones who had to start the cooking fire every day," Aline began, glancing at Ziada. "It was really hard, and we were only little kids. We would squat on the ground. In the center of the charcoal we'd light a plastic bag and let it burn, hoping the charcoal would catch fire." In my nose I could imagine the acrid smell of plastic burning. I pictured Aline and Ziada blowing desperately on the flames, as black smoke rushed into their faces.

Aline suddenly stopped the story and looked at me skeptically.

"Dada, do you know what I mean by charcoal?"

Aline had stumbled on a word that in translation loses its meaning. She was talking about the charred pieces of wood that I had seen carried in bundles on the top of women's heads throughout Goma. Congolese charcoal bore little resemblance to Canada's uniformly sized bricks, perfectly dry, and drenched with lighter fluid. Congolese charcoal was often very hard to light.

Aline continued, "Sometimes the charcoal was no good, and the fire would go out. Sometimes when we got the fire going, flames would leap out at us. It would burn us, and the ashes would fly into our eyes. Sometimes our heads would go dizzy from trying to blow on the flames."

Ziada jumped in. "Oh my God! Sometimes we had to try and start the fire ten times. And then, even then, it would fail." Ziada paused as if remembering a scene from a movie, then she continued. "The worst part was that if we couldn't get the fire going, we would have to walk to the other houses nearby and ask if they had any burning coals we could take. Sometimes, there were people that just didn't want to give us any. Finally, if someone gave us some burning coals, we would pile them on the metal lid of a pan. Then we would try to make our way home, balancing the lid on the edge of our fingertips, knowing if we walked too slowly the hot metal would start to burn our fingers, and if we walked too fast, the coals would spill from the lid, onto the ground in front of us, burning our feet."

Aline and Ziada were acting out the scene now, their fingers holding imaginary metal lids, their feet tiptoeing carefully.

Aline and Ziada were speaking in Swahili even though their English was astonishingly good. I translated their story into English and typed it into my laptop, then read it back to them. Their faces lit up in recognition of their own lives on the page. Ziada let loose with her barrel laugh. "Yes! That's it! That's it exactly!" she exclaimed. "So funny! So funny!"

Then they turned serious. "What about the water? You didn't write about carrying the water!" Aline pointed out, a shadow darting across her face.

"Okay, tell me about carrying water," I said.

"The water containers were so heavy," Aline started out in English, then shook her head and switched back into Swahili. She recounted how they would get up at 4:00 AM to fetch water before school. Down the hill, in the dark, groups of children would climb for an hour until they reached the edge of the lake. Then they would wade into the lake to fill up their giant containers, so they could bring home water to wash dishes, cook and bathe.

"We had to be careful," Aline continued. "Sometimes a wave would rush in and carry away our water containers. Sometimes kids drowned—trying to save their containers."

Aline and Ziada went on to describe the long walk home, laden down with water. They described how they would tie a cloth around their foreheads, then harness the yellow containers to the cloth, allowing them to hang down their backs, like a backwards necklace, roughly twenty kilograms (forty-four pounds) too heavy.

"The worst part was the hills," Ziada said. "We had to lean into the hills so that we wouldn't topple backwards."

Then she described the time when the cloth around her forehead slipped. Her head snapped backward in pain and her water container crashed to the ground and tumbled back down the hill. "I stood there on that hill, my neck aching, knowing that I had to start all over again," Ziada said, shaking her head.

Ziada and Aline both paused and stared at me. "Wait, maybe you don't understand," Aline said, suddenly animated. She went to the refrigerator and returned with gallons of milk. Then she tied a cloth around her forehead and hung one container of milk down her back. She put another gallon on top of her head to demonstrate how they would walk, balancing two containers at once. Aline was standing in her apartment in Canada, but the image carried me back to Congo. I could imagine her feet on lava rock, climbing up hills. I could feel the weight of the water container, six times heavier than this milk jug.

"One day, I tried to tell my class about how we would carry water in Africa. Some people didn't believe me," Aline said, her face suddenly crestfallen. "It is so different here in Canada, sometimes it is hard to explain."

"One day you will write your own books," I responded.

"Actually, we're going to make a movie," Aline said without a pause. Then the two girls began to laugh again.

CHAPTER NINETY-SIX

Right with the World

July 2018

In the summer of 2018, I brought my family to Canada to stay for a month. "These are our friends from Congo," I told my six-year-old daughter on the day we arrived in Canada.

All her life, my daughter has worn African dresses sent to her from someone far away. She's seen brightly colored bags stacked around our house. "Hello, Little Neema," voices have called out to her from long-distance phone lines while she hid her face in embarrassment.

But now, we were finally together.

My daughter and I climbed up the stairs to Mapendo's apartment. Mapendo's oldest son, Jonathan, is just half a year younger than my daughter. Watching the two of them play together gave me more satisfaction than I can explain. They raced around the parking lot with bicycles, tricycles, and scooters. Jonathan already knew how to ride a two-wheel bike, and he cruised around the parking lot fearlessly.

"Just go like this, Neema," he said to my daughter in crisp English. My daughter was still leaning on training wheels that slowed her down. She circled her legs as fast as she could to keep up.

Later that evening, when the children rushed back inside Mapendo's apartment, my daughter came to me, hot and sweaty in the summer air, and whispered a secret in my ear. "I am going to ride a bike like Jonathan someday," she said.

For a moment, sitting there at Mapendo's table, our children side by side, and the future stretching out equally before all of them, everything finally seemed right with the world.

CHAPTER NINETY-SEVEN

A Little More

Mapendo's kitchen table was loaded down with bowls of food at mealtimes. There were bowls of beans and rice. There was a sauce with eggplant and fish. And there were always plates of ugali. Ugali is corn meal or cassava flour that is formed into large balls of dough. The rounded balls of dough sat on a plate in the center of the table, looking kind of like yellowish playdough. We each reached toward the plate, and broke off some of the dough, then dipped it into the sauce in our bowls. "It's not dinner without ugali," Argentine said.

We sat there sharing our food as we had done so many years before.

After a while, Mapendo looked suspiciously at my bowl. "Dada, haukule hata," Mapendo said in Swahili. "Sister, you are not even eating,"

"Ndiyo! Ninakula!" I insisted. "Yes! I am eating!

I finished my bowl and turned towards Argentine, who was laughing about something. When I turned back to my empty bowl, it was full again.

At the end of the meal, Ziada returned with a pitcher of water and a plastic basin. One after another, we put our hands over the plastic basin, and Ziada poured warm water over our hands.

At the end of summer, when we go back to my house in New York, my parents will come to visit, and we'll sit at our table. "Wait, wait!" my daughter will say, racing into the kitchen and emerging with a plastic bowl and a pitcher full of water. "Put your hands out," she will instruct her grandparents. "We have to wash our hands." After her grandparents have washed their hands, my daughter will return the plastic bowl and the pitcher to the kitchen. "That is how they do it in Canada," she will say proudly.

CHAPTER NINETY-EIGHT

Three Signatures

August 2018

"Tuende. Tuende mbiyo."—"Let's go. Let's go quickly," I said to Argentine and Mapendo. It was a hot day in August, and I wanted to get to this particular office in Athabasca before it closed.

We arrived at the nondescript building just in time. We were bearing all our identification plus Can$475. There were cement stairs leading to the office, and Argentine and Mapendo clung to the railing and hoisted themselves up one step at a time.

"Don't worry. It will be worth it," I said.

We sat in that office and signed papers incorporating SHONA Congo Sewing Ltd. in Canada. "We *all* have to sign," I said, and we lined up our three signatures, one after another.

It was the first time we had been able to do this officially, to incorporate a business together. I felt immensely proud to have Argentine and Mapendo as partners, and to see our partnership finally written on paper.

CHAPTER NINETY-NINE

The Farmers Market

While I was in Athabasca that summer, I accompanied Argentine and Mapendo to the Athabasca farmers market every Saturday. One of the girls came with us as well. We carried a folding table and a pop-up tent that often threatened to blow away. We piled our belongings on the pavement, waved at Yvonne, the market manager, and joined the other vendors in the parking lot by the river. There were vendors who carved wood and others who sold cookies. There was a family from Syria selling hummus and a woman from Turkey selling spinach pies.

We hung our bags from racks at the front of the tent and set up the folding table and chairs inside.

"Welcome, welcome," Argentine called out to everyone who passed by. Sometimes the people passing by couldn't even see Argentine; she was so small that she disappeared behind the stacks of cloth on the table where she was seated. But her voice always rang out with an enthusiastic welcome.

"Welcome, Grandma!" Argentine called out to an older woman walking by. I opened my mouth and started to explain that a stranger might not prefer the title of Grandma. But after a few words, I stopped. Argentine had already moved on to the next person, greeting each stranger with titles that reflected personal relationships. "Hello, Mommy!" she said to a younger woman. "Hello, Baby!" she said to a three-year-old boy.

The three-year-old boy paused, staring at Argentine. With Argentine sitting in her chair, the two of them were eye-to-eye. Argentine caught his gaze. "Can you share your cookie with me?" Argentine asked the little boy. He turned to his mother, surprised by the question, cookie halfway to his mouth.

Argentine doesn't really like cookies. She doesn't like sweetness except in her tea. But she carried on the conversation with all her heart. "Maybe just one bite? Yes? Can you share with me? Please?"

The little boy and his mother moved on, and the little boy kept a firm grip on his cookie. But as they walked away, I could hear the mother whispering in his ear, "It's good to share."

Standing there in the market in Athabasca, Argentine reminded me of someone else. In her voice I could hear the same tone that I heard in Mama Kavira's voice many years ago. "Mzungu, did you buy bread for me at the market today?" Mama Kavira had asked that question of me repeatedly.

And now here was Argentine asking her own version of the same question—the same invitation.

As the day wore on, Argentine kept calling out to people passing by. Her greetings were both beautiful and slightly alarming. "Hello, Grandma!" "Hello, Sister!" I thought of the way that, for Argentine, every relationship was personal, every woman walking by was a potential sister, mother or grandma. In Argentine's world, we are all connected.

CHAPTER ONE HUNDRED

Favorite Colors

On a warm summer day, Argentine, Mapendo and I went to Gaskia African Fashions in Edmonton. Mama Ayina, the store's owner, came running out from behind the counter. "They're here! They're here," she said, wrapping us all in hugs. Kate and I had stopped by the shop many months before, on the cold day in December when Argentine and Mapendo arrived at the airport. But now it was summer, and we were back.

"What colors will you choose today?" Mama Ayina asked with a sparkle in her eye.

"Pink! Pink!" Argentine declared confidently. "Dada, you know people love pink, don't you?"

Mapendo held up a turquoise cloth with big flower designs in violet. Argentine and I began debating the challenges of such a large design. "Maybe if we cut it like this..." Argentine started to say, reaching for the cloth. But the cloth was already gone. Mapendo had quietly tucked it into our "yes" pile with no further consultation. "This one we are getting," she said in that steady voice of hers.

I looked at my own stack of favorite fabrics, noticing that I had chosen almost entirely blue and green. *It's okay,* I thought to myself. *When we put our favorite colors together, they make a whole rainbow.*

The following week, at the market, each of us watched our own favorite colors, running a friendly competition of sorts. "See, I told you people would love pink!" Argentine exclaimed every time someone chose her fabric.

Mapendo's bags with the giant violet flowers sold out quickly. "Congratulations!" we said to Mapendo.

"Dada, did you know our customers really look at the quality? They check the zippers, pulling them open and closed. They flip the bag inside and out to see how well we sewed," Argentine said shaking her head in amazement.

I decided to seize the moment to emphasize an issue. "You know Argentine, we also really need price tags on our bags. People are afraid to buy the bags if they can't see the price." I'd been trying for a while to convince Argentine and Mapendo on the importance of how we displayed our products.

Argentine nodded. "Ndiyo, dada," she said solemnly. "Yes, sister."

I smiled, satisfied that I had convinced her on the value of price tags. Then, after a few minutes, Argentine turned back to me, flashing her brilliant smile.

"Wenye wako na roho kuuza, watauza." Her comment translated to "Those who have a heart to buy the bags, will buy the bags."

In brilliant Argentine style, I couldn't tell whether she had just issued a dismissal of my entire argument or a beautiful statement of faith. Perhaps it was both.

CHAPTER ONE HUNDRED AND ONE

Moambe Chicken

Later on that day, two women stopped by our tent at the market. Argentine and Mapendo welcomed them, showing off bags. "This one is reversible. This one has a zipper," Mapendo said in English.

The women listened carefully and then walked on, promising to read our website and return another week.

They returned ten minutes later. "There was just something that pulled us back here," they said, buying their first of many SHONA bags. We saw them again the next week, and the week after that. They arranged to come to Mapendo's apartment one day so they could order custom-made African outfits.

One of the sisters began looking up how to say things in Swahili, sending Mapendo text messages that read "Jambo" and "Habari gani." The other sister began cooking Congolese recipes. "I found a recipe for Moambe chicken," she reported with excitement.

The two women sat down at Mapendo's kitchen table. "Tell us about life in Congo," they said. There was a pause as Argentine and Mapendo searched for English words to capture their lives. The pause went on for a while, and maybe someone would say it was awkward. But sitting there at the table with these four women bravely smiling back and forth at each other, I knew these were the conversations where friendships were built.

CHAPTER ONE HUNDRED AND TWO

Squash Greens

Whenever they were at the farmers market, Argentine and Mapendo always eyed the produce from across the market, studying the displays for their favorite vegetables. "We got potatoes from here," Argentine reported. "They were so fresh and delicious, just like in Masisi."

One day after the market had closed, a green leaf caught Argentine's eye. It wasn't on a vendor's table but planted in a garden at the center of the roundabout where the market was set up. I had walked by that roundabout countless times and seen it only as landscaping. But it was a garden, replete with tomatoes and onions and such.

"Are those squash greens?" Argentine whispered to Mapendo, pointing at a green leaf growing in the garden. Mapendo stopped to look.

"Neema," Mapendo whispered, "go check those leaves. See if they are squash leaves."

Neema stopped folding the bags and turned to Mapendo.

"Really? You want me to jump into that garden there and see if those are squash leaves?" Neema replied.

"Ndiyo! Fanya mbiyo!" Mapendo exclaimed. "Yes!! Do it quickly!"

Neema went, slowly at first, working her way casually to the center of the garden. She bent down and picked one of the prickly leaves, smiling in recognition. Soon she had a whole handful. Other vendors began passing by, packing up their own cars for the day. They stopped to watch.

"What are you doing?" one woman called out.

"I am picking these leaves here," Neema replied. The woman's eyes grew wide.

"What will you do with the leaves?" another woman asked.

"They make a very delicious soup."

The women smiled over at Neema. "That is very smart of you. You must teach us how to cook that soup one day."

I asked Neema later about that story.

"Were you embarrassed to go and pick the leaves from that garden in the roundabout?"

"Well, yes, of course I was embarrassed," she replied with a smile. "But...squash greens are delicious, and it had been a long time since I had tasted them."

CHAPTER ONE HUNDRED AND THREE

Memorizing the Roads

Near the end of the summer, Argentine and Mapendo begged me to take them on one more trip to Edmonton where they could buy smoked fish and cooking bananas. I finally agreed. My phone's GPS didn't work well in Canada, and I asked Argentine and Mapendo if they knew the way. Argentine, in the back seat, laughed. "I could never follow these roads," she said.

"I know the way," Mapendo interrupted, her face set into a determined expression. She pointed at an intersection, "Turn here."

Some of my Canadian friends had mentioned that Mapendo was often quiet in car rides. They wondered if she might be sad or lonely or struggling with English. Watching her, as she pointed me down the road, I realized that for all her quiet car trips, Mapendo had been looking out the window, memorizing roads.

"Really? You have memorized the roads!" I said to Mapendo. She looked back at me, proudly. "Maybe one day I will drive my own car," she said.

CHAPTER ONE HUNDRED AND FOUR

New Life

April 2019

On April 2, 2019, Mapendo and Joseph's third son was born. Baby Josaphat was born in Canada, sixteen months after his parents arrived.

Mapendo gave birth to her son in a country that was still foreign to her. She was still learning the language. The tastes of a new country still prickled her tongue. "At the hospital they fed me Canadian food, and I ate it!" Mapendo said in a miniature celebration.

Every time I ask Mapendo if she is happy that she came to Canada, she looks at me quizzically. "Yes, of course," she says. "There is no war here. And the children go to school every day."

Mapendo was scheduled for a c-section. She was told to arrive at the hospital first thing in the morning. A friend from church arrived at 4 AM to drive Mapendo and Joseph to the hospital that morning.

In Congo, childbirth is the domain of women. A pregnant mother arrives at the hospital with a female relative to help care for her. At first, Mapendo had thought that Neema might accompany her to the hospital in Canada. But the logistics of school and new cultural expectations prevailed. Joseph accompanied Mapendo to the hospital.

That morning I texted Joseph to see how everything was going. "They just started the anesthesia," Joseph reported. "I don't know what to do with myself. I have to hide in the restroom just to pray."

After the baby was born, Mapendo stayed in recovery for three or four hours. A nurse pulled Joseph aside. "Put this gown on," the nurse said. Joseph tried to put the gown over his shirt, but the nurse told him to take his shirt off.

In Goma, men aren't allowed to go into the maternity ward. For those first days of new life, babies are surrounded by women. Joseph held his first two sons only after they were released from the hospital, a week after they were born.

Now, minutes after his third son was born, here was Joseph in a paper gown. A nurse came in with a tiny baby in her arms. She pulled the gown down from Joseph's chest, pressing the baby skin-to-skin.

A few days later, when they came home from the hospital, Argentine called me, sitting at the table with Joseph and Mapendo. They were celebrating the new baby. "Felicitations!" I shouted over the phone line. "Congratulations!"

I heard laughter punctuating the air and the excited voices of children in the background. The baby cried and Mapendo nursed him. Then I heard Joseph picking up his son and talking to him like an old friend. Soon the baby was back to sleep.

Mapendo and Joseph talked of this birth in tones I hadn't heard before. At the hospital in Canada, Mapendo and Joseph stumbled together through the uncertainty of a new culture. "I got so scared and so cold when they gave me the anesthesia. I couldn't feel it working. It wasn't the same as Congo. I didn't know what would happen," Mapendo explained.

I asked Mapendo which of her son's births had scared her the most, thinking of that midnight walk in Goma for Jonathan's birth. "This one in Canada," she answered quickly.

"Oh yes! This one was so scary!" Joseph chimed in. "Everything is so new for us here. But we do our best. We just try and accommodate ourselves to all the new things," Joseph said.

Sometimes I think of all that my friends have gained and all that they have lost. It is an equation that I can never figure out how to balance—like apples and oranges—the numbers refuse to compute.

Joseph's father died unexpectedly in Congo only a few months after Joseph and his family arrived in Canada. When I called Joseph and Mapendo to offer my sympathy, I found that Argentine had spent the whole night in Mapendo and Joseph's apartment—a few doors down from her own. In the tradition of Congo, the two families had sung and prayed through the night.

A few months after Josaphat was born, Mapendo's mother and sister went missing. For days Mapendo had no idea where they were. She called up friends in Goma and sent neighbors to look for them. Their houses had been attacked by thieves. They had fled with nothing. *Where had they gone? How far could they have gotten?* Mapendo's mother was in no condition to travel, even under better circumstances.

The days passed slowly. Mapendo sat in her apartment in Canada nursing her baby. She prayed for her mother. She cut cloth, and she sewed. She stared at her phone, waiting for news, carrying a burden that nobody could see. Finally, she received news that her mother had been found, sick, at the refugee transit camp just over the border in Uganda. Mapendo's sister (Neema and Ziada's mother) was with her in the refugee camp. So were Neema and Ziada's siblings.

"I never wanted my mother to flee. I know how difficult the road is. I know how hard life is in the refugee camps. I don't know if my mother's body is strong enough for that," Mapendo whispered to me over the phone one day.

In the background of our conversation I heard the baby cooing, the sounds of new life filled Mapendo's apartment—like a river forever pulling her forward.

I wonder if this newborn baby will ever meet his grandma.

I hope so. I hope that one day Mapendo's family comes back together again.

CHAPTER ONE HUNDRED AND FIVE

Without Walls

SHONA Congo continues long distance, with Riziki and Solange in Goma, Argentine and Mapendo in Athabasca, and me in New York. A few years ago, I moved from Brooklyn to a small town in upstate New York.

Moving to this new town has proven surprisingly like moving to Congo. I find myself facing the same question here that I faced long ago in Goma. *How can I live without too many walls?* In Goma, the question was visceral—I faced it every time I passed the guards at our gate. Here it is easier for me to miss the many walls that surround me—the invisible ones that keep me primarily talking to people whose lives look like my own. The truth is that right here in my little town, like in most places these days, there are a surprising number of people from different countries, different cultures, different economic backgrounds, and different worldviews. There are so many people whose lives I haven't yet created the time or the space to acknowledge.

In honor of Congo, I am trying to slow down. To let go of efficiency. To walk instead of ride. To call out to my neighbors. To share a plate of food with someone I don't know. And, most of all, to lean my head back and laugh.

CHAPTER ONE HUNDRED AND SIX

Over the Ocean

When I moved to eastern Congo twelve years ago, I feared an erupting volcano and an exploding lake. Leaving for Canada last year, Argentine feared an airplane. Mapendo, Joseph, and Argentine still laugh, remembering how scared Argentine was on those planes on the way to Canada.

"She prayed so hard and so loud that her prayers are still hanging out there, mid-air, spread out over the ocean," Joseph says.

I like that image—prayers spread out over the ocean. If only we could leave our fears there too.

There is so much to fear these days. I think of my own country racked with fear. We fear losing our jobs. We fear immigrants. We fear ourselves.

There is plenty to fear in Congo too. The people of Goma live in the space between one danger and another—one fear and another. It is an incredibly difficult way to live. And yet, I wonder what we might learn from the people of Goma.

Mapendo once said, "In Goma, we had to pull ourselves toward each other. We had no other choice."

Perhaps in the United States we think we have too many other options. We have come to believe in the myth of self-built security, as though security can exist apart from community.

In truth, community is what I have been seeking all along. And fear is what has gotten in the way. The problem has not been Argentine and Mapendo's fears, but my own. During most of our friendship, they lived constantly on the edge of disaster. In the face of one crisis after another, they would surrender themselves, shaking their heads, saying, "Mungu atatusaidia." "God will help us." But I would hold on too tightly, white knuckling our way forward, trying to fix a future that had yet to arrive.

In my wildest dreams I could never have imagined this future. Aline serves pancakes and sings pop songs. Jonathan races his bicycle next to my daughter. The future is sometimes glaringly bright. But then I see that which is familiar. Argentine and Mapendo stand at a table and cut African cloth. They still sew every day. And at night they still close their eyes and dream of a perfect future; one in which all the people they love are safe.

Argentine and Mapendo are enormously grateful to live in Canada. "We've finally reached a place where we can stop running," Argentine says. "We've come from so far," Mapendo whispers in a tone of wonder.

Yet their phones still beep with calls from Africa. It can feel as though the needs in Congo and in the refugee camps will never end. Nor will the dangers. Argentine and Mapendo answer the calls from their families, listening to stories of disaster, sending money when they can, and praying always.

And then they surrender their fears. They put their phones down and head out to parent-teacher night at the local Athabasca schools. They marvel at the shiny new buildings and the opportunities these schools hold for their children. They go to English classes and return home to cook beans. They welcome anyone who walks through the door. They step carefully between one world and another.

I've learned to let go a bit, to surrender myself. I've learned that, in the face of fear, sometimes the only thing left to do is to pull ourselves toward each other. The people of Goma live by an exploding lake, at the base of an active volcano, in the middle of war and poverty. But the weather is perfect, music pumps from the street-side shops, and people will always call out, "Karibu kwetu." "Welcome to our home."

Epilogue

- Mapendo continues to live in Athabasca with her husband, three sons, and two nieces.
- Mapendo's mother is currently in a refugee camp in Uganda along with Neema and Ziada's mother and siblings. Four of Joseph's siblings are living in a refugee camp in Burundi.
- In June 2019, Neema completed Grade 10, Ziada completed Grade 7, Jonathan completed grade 1, and Joachim completed Kindergarten in Athabasca. They are all doing well in school.
- Joseph works in Athabasca and diligently continues his studies online.
- Argentine continues to live in Atahabasca with her younger sister and daughter.
- In June 2019 Aline completed Grade 8. She won a singing competition at her school and was awarded the opportunity to sing on the main stage at a summer festival in Athabasca on Canada Day.
- Argentine and Aline's parents and most of their siblings are living in a refugee camp in Uganda.
- Rachelle's body is buried in Goma, but we carry her spirit and her memory with us always.
- Riziki and Solange continue to live in Goma with their husbands and children. They each have three children. They continue to sew for SHONA and receive

100% of the estimated profit from every item they sew. They ask for your prayers for their safety.

- Argentine, Mapendo, and Dawn are co-owners of SHONA Congo Sewing Ltd in Canada.
- According to Human Rights Watch, in 2018 there were more than 140 armed groups active in eastern Congo. 4.5 million people in Congo are displaced from their homes due to clashes among armed groups and government forces. More than 13 million Congolese people are in need of humanitarian assistance.
- UNHCR estimates that as of 2018 there were 25.9 million refugees worldwide. In 2016, there were 126,000 refugee resettlement spaces worldwide. By 2018, that number had been reduced to 51,000. In the United States, President Trump capped the number of refugees who that can be resettled in the United States at 30,000 for 2019, causing drastic reductions in funding for refugee resettlement organizations in the United States. For the year 2020, the administration has floated the possibility of accepting zero refugees into the United States.
- In July of 2019 the first case of Ebola was confirmed in the city of Goma. The World Health Organization declared the Ebola epidemic a global health emergency less than a week later. The people of Goma continue to live in the space between one danger and another.

Author's Note

This book is based on our lives. No matter how hard I try to get everything right, there will be mistakes. Nothing is ever complete. Some pieces of Argentine and Mapendo's lives don't translate easily. And some pieces of their lives I have yet to fully understand. In the landscape of Congo, Burundi and Uganda, I am still learning.

And yet I have done the best I can. I have retold in English the stories that my friends have told me in Swahili. Because I believe their perspective is worth sharing. Argentine and Mapendo have taught me to see the world differently. And I can only pray that this book has given you that opportunity as well.

This book was written over cups of tea at the kitchen table, amid much joy and laughter. With Argentine starting one story and Mapendo breaking in halfway through, and the whole effort devolving into debate and laughter—chasing memories that are strikingly immediate yet forever just out of reach.

Sometimes, in the writing of this book, I have also brought my friends to tears. "Nisamehe," I have said. "Forgive me." What else can I say for returning my friends to the painful memories that are seared on their hearts?

One time, Joseph responded, "But we cannot forget these memories anyway. How can we forget them? They are realities that our people are still living."

And so, we trust these memories to you, in honor of all those that live in this reality every day.

Joseph's father walked over one hundred kilometers, then traveled by bus, to see his grandchildren one last time. When he saw them, he anointed his grandchildren with oil. He prayed that wherever they went, those who welcomed them would be blessed. And then he begged not to be forgotten.

And so, collectively, we answer Joseph's father. We answer Mapendo's mother. Argentine's mother. Neema and Ziada's mother. Riziki and Solange. "Usinisahau," they each said. "Don't forget me." "Hatutakusahau," we answer. "We will not forget you."

Learn More at www.shonacongo.com

See pictures and videos
from every part of this journey.

Learn more about the many topics
referred to in this book.

Buy the bags handcrafted by
Argentine, Mapendo, Riziki, & Solange
10% off your next order
Discount code: book185

Shukrani

To Argentine, Mapendo, Joseph, Neema, Aline, Ziada, Asante Mungu, Jonathan, Joachim, and Josaphat: *Thank you for sharing your lives with me. I am forever grateful for your friendship.*

To the people of Goma: *Thank you for welcoming me to your community.*

To all the supporters of SHONA Congo: *We would not be where we are without your help. Thank you for believing in us.*

To AIRSS, to their supporters, and to the people of Athabasca and beyond: *Thank you for welcoming newcomers to your community and thank you for the countless ways that you support them.*

To my ESOL students: I *pray that one day we live in a world that recognizes the hard work, generosity, and beauty that each of you has brought to this country.*

To my husband: *Thank you for sharing every part of this journey with me. I love you, and I love our life together.*

To my parents: *Thank you for your unwavering love and support. You give me the courage to follow my dreams.*

To my mother-in-law and father-in-law: *Thank you for your faithful lives in Rwanda and Burundi (and Kansas too). You have inspired me and taught me so much.*

To my daughter*: I love you to the moon and back.*

To Cheryl, Joe, and Sam: *Thank you for carefully reading countless versions of this book.*

To my editor, Luke Gerwe, and my graphic designer, Robin Locke: *Thank you for your patience, hard work and wisdom. And thank you for believing in this project.*

Argentine and Mapendo would like to thank God, and they would like to thank their mothers, for loving and carrying them always.

Discussion Questions

Part I

1. The majority of Part I takes place in the city of Goma. What are some of the positive aspects of life in Goma? What are some of difficulties?
2. The story of Mama Kavira and the bread provides a touchstone throughout the book. What do you think the incident is really about?
3. Argentine and Mapendo both face difficult childhoods. In what ways do they face similar challenges? In what ways do they face different challenges?
4. What do you think are the primary lessons that Argentine and Mapendo might have learned from their experiences in Part I?
5. What do you think are the primary lessons that Dawn has learned in Part I?

Part II

6. This part of the book is dedicated to describing the many ways that Argentine and Mapendo are displaced from their homes (fleeing around the lake, fleeing to Burundi, fleeing to Uganda). In what ways do their experiences of displacement look different than you might have imagined?
7. How does the author's friendship with Argentine and Mapendo change during this section?

8. It could be said that this is a book about motherhood. Discuss the role of mothers in Part I and Part II.
9. What surprised you about the refugee camps in Burundi and Uganda? What are some of the biggest challenges that Argentine and Mapendo faced in those camps?
10. Before reading Part III, what did you anticipate might be some of the biggest challenges that Argentine and Mapendo and their families would face in Canada.

Part III

11. What are some of the things that Argentine, Mapendo and their families seem to appreciate most about Canada? What are some of the challenges they face?
12. At the end of chapter ninety-three the author writes, "I see Aline, Ziada, and Neema poised with their toes pressed to the edge of this line, trying their best to hold it all together; to make sense of a world that offers vastly different futures to some of its children than to others." What are some ways that you see this disparity in the world? How do you see it in your own community?
13. What is your favorite story from Part III and why?
14. In what ways do the lives that Argentine and Mapendo build in Canada reflect Congolese culture and values? In what ways do they seem to have changed to adapt to life in Canada?
15. In the end of the book the author writes, "Mapendo once said, 'In Goma we learned to pull ourselves toward each other. We had no other choice.'" Looking at Argentine and Mapendo's experiences throughout this book, in what ways has their security and safety been tied to community?

16. In reference to the United States, the author concludes, "We have come to believe in the myth of self-built security, as though security can exist apart from community." In what ways would you say this is true or untrue in the context where you live?
17. What was your biggest take-away from this book?

Made in the USA
Lexington, KY
29 November 2019